How much do you really
True or Fa

1. A handwritten will is just as valid as a typewritten one.   T   F
2. A "no-contest" clause can effectively deter someone from challenging a will.   T   F
3. Any property you own can be transferred by a will.   T   F
4. If you're part owner of a house, your spouse has a legal right to inherit your share.   T   F
5. You can disinherit anyone you want to.   T   F
6. If you leave money to minor children, there's no way to prevent them from squandering it when they turn eighteen.   T   F
7. Naming a guardian for your children will keep your ex from getting custody of them.   T   F
8. If you're going to leave unequal shares of your estate to your children, it's smart to tell them why.   T   F
9. Videotaping the signing of a will can prove the signer is "of sound mind."   T   F
10. If you die without a will, your spouse automatically inherits everything after taxes.   T   F

Answers. 1. F (see p. 14), 2. T (see p. 59), 3. F (see p. 16), 4. F (see p. 18), 5. F (see p. 19), 6. F (see p. 102), 7. F (see p. 26), 8. T (see p. 43), 9. T (see p. 58), 10. F (see p. 7)

What Your Lawyer
May *Not* Tell You About

YOUR
FAMILY'S
WILL

*A Guide to Preventing the Common
Pitfalls That Can Lead to Family Fights*

Kaja Whitehouse

NEW YORK   BOSTON

Warner Business Books
Warner Books

Time Warner Book Group
1271 Avenue of the Americas, New York, NY 10020
Visit our Web site at www.twbookmark.com.

The Warner Business Books logo is a trademark of Warner Books.

Printed in the United States of America

First Edition: March 2006

10 9 8 7 6 5 4 3 2 1

Library of Congress Cataloging-in-Publication Data

Whitehouse, Kaja.
    What your lawyer may not tell you about your family's will : a guide to preventing the common pitfalls that can lead to family fights / Kaja Whitehouse.—1st ed.
        p. cm.
    Summary: "Written for the lay person who wants to know the basics regarding one's will, as well one's legal rights when it comes to the wills of family members."— Provided by the publisher.
    ISBN-13: 978-0-446-69545-9
    ISBN-10: 0-446-69545-9
    1. Wills—United States—Popular works. 2. Inheritance and succession—United States—Popular works. I. Title.
    KF755.Z9W49 2006
    346.7305'4—dc22

                                                                        2005023697

Cover design by Erin Sharpe
Cover photo by Dennis O'Clair/Getty Images
Book design by Charles Sutherland

To Yeye, a unique soul I knew in life
and
Nancy, a pretty face I knew afterward

ACKNOWLEDGMENTS

I would like to extend a special thanks to my family and everyone at Dow Jones Newswires for their support. I would also like to thank all the people who shared their personal estate planning stories for this book.

Legal assistance was provided by Philip V. Bouklas, an attorney with Agins, Siegel & Reiner, LLP in New York, and Geoff R. Casavant, an independent practitioner in Houston. Additional assistance was provided by Ted Kurlowicz, a professor of taxation and estate planning at The American College in Bryn Mawr, Pennsylvania, and his spouse, Alex Kurlowicz, an insurance agent and registered representative. Egan Lo, Esq., provided editorial assistance.

CONTENTS

Contents

PART II: ADVANCED PLANNING

PART III: WRAPPING THINGS UP

Contents

HOW TO USE THIS BOOK

This book is an introduction to wills and estate planning for people who know nothing or very little about the subject. I'll start off with information about why you want to plan for your death and how you can go about creating this plan. I'll explain what to look for when you're planning for and drafting a will and other wealth transfer instruments. Later, I'll touch on more complex planning strategies such as trusts and planning for incapacity.

This book also explores some of the emotional issues that commonly crop up in death planning: *Can I cut people out of my will? Can I control how my heirs spend their inheritance? Should I give more to the child who needs it the most?*

Along the way, you will be introduced to real people who have shared their stories about common mistakes in estate planning. I hope these stories—along with a few hypothetical examples and some case law—will help you better grasp the sometimes obscure and complex rules of estate planning. While a few of the stories in this book were pulled from case law and ripped from the headlines, most were offered voluntarily by people who wanted to share their experiences and lessons. I've thus disguised their identities, for privacy reasons.

Despite the title, the point of this book isn't to demonize

lawyers. Indeed, many lawyers helped out in the crafting of this book, and they may help you in drafting or executing your plan. The point is to make you aware of the laws and pitfalls that you might encounter before you decide whether and what kind of professional advice—if any—is right for you.

No one expects you to read this book cover to cover. (If you do, way to go!) Rather, it's intended to act as a resource. Feel free to skip chapters or to revisit those you skipped at a later date. If your children are grown, for example, you may want to skip the section on planning for the care of minor children. If you already have a will but want to consider adding a trust, you may want to pass over the section on wills.

Since the book is structured as a resource, information is sometimes repeated from one chapter to another. I want to make sure that readers who skip chapter 1, for example, are still made aware that the state will decide who gets what if you die without a will.

Also, the information provided within this book is not state-specific—nor should it be. I've given some examples of how certain states do things, but I cannot cover the laws of every state. Individual state rules on wills, trusts, property rights, and much more can vary from what you'll find in this book. As you'll learn (several times), you'll want to research the exact rules of your state before implementing your plan—or at least hire a lawyer who can do this for you.

To make certain information easier to find, pay special attention to the following when they come up:

- **LOOK OUT!:** Alerts you to common mistakes or misunderstandings.
- **TECH TALK:** Digs deeper into the explanation of certain concepts.
- **DICTIONARY:** Provides definitions of important terms.

PART I

THE BASICS

Everyone will die someday. As your time nears, you will probably ask yourself many questions: *Did I live my life to the fullest? Do I have any regrets? Will my family be okay without me?*

This book can't help you resolve the first two questions. Those are personal issues you should be dealing with throughout your life. But it can help you with the last question: *Will my family be okay without me?*

With proper planning, you can ensure that your family is taken care of, both physically and financially. In other words, you can try to limit the pain they feel following your death to their mourning. Without proper planning, you might expose them to the pain of mourning combined with legal burdens, family fights, or a lack of funds to pay the bills.

This type of planning is called estate planning. Yes, it's a vague and slightly highfalutin term that evokes images of Scarlett O'Hara waltzing about her plantation. But estate planning doesn't have to be highfalutin or complex. Your plan can consist of a few simple documents, including a simple will, health care instructions in case of brain damage or terminal illness, and funeral instructions. You can even construct the plan in the comfort of your own home, without the help of an attorney. A lot of people, especially younger people, start off with relatively straightforward plans involving a simple will and nothing more. You can always add to your plan down the road as you think necessary.

Certainly, it's important to know what you can do with your estate plan, even if you choose not to take advantage of all your options. The first step is to brush up on the basics of estate planning. In this section, you will learn about wills—the centerpiece of any estate plan. I'll tell you what makes a will legal, as well as the legal limitations of wills. You will also learn how to assess your estate according to the laws that govern property, and how to protect your will against disgruntled heirs.

Behind all this technical talk, however, I'll be touching upon the human elements of estate planning. After all, behind any estate plan are very basic human concerns, such as:

- Who gets your money if you die without a plan?
- How do you ensure that your wishes are followed?
- Who will take care of your minor children if both parents die?
- Can you give more to the child you think needs it the most?
- What do you do if you want to cut someone out of your will?
- What happens to your personal stuff, such as a book collection, if nobody wants it?

Chapter 1

THE IMPORTANCE OF PLANNING

When You Don't Plan, You Let the Courts Decide

Most people are reasonable and know that an estate or inheritance plan is important. Still, it's hard to take the time to make it happen. Why? Well, the term *estate planning* generally leads to images of sitting around a lawyer's office discussing the many ways you might die, and the many things that might happen to your heirs and assets when you do. As if that weren't uncomfortable enough, it also means taking the time to draft, organize, and sign the legal documents, such as wills and trusts, that dictate who will get what when you die. A trip to the dentist is almost more appealing.

There is also a sense of futility to inheritance planning. After all, why plan for something you will never see to fruition? Even worse, some people believe that planning for death is akin to inviting death to the door.

One thing that can help get procrastinators back on track, however, is knowing what might happen to their heirs and their assets when they don't plan, or when they plan poorly. When you don't plan, you let the state decide who gets what. That means the court system will distribute your assets according to predetermined laws and decide who gets to take care of your minor children.

Who Gets My Money if I Die Without a Plan?

To learn what might happen if you don't plan, take a look at Frank's story. Frank was a fun-loving guy who never drafted a will. He wasn't married and had no kids, so he didn't see the need. Also, while Frank worked hard enough to live and play, he never really had a lot of money.

All that changed, however, when Frank suffered an accident on the job. He damaged his spinal cord and several of his vertebrae. His doctors said he would never regain full control of his body movements. His suffering resulted in $6 million in damages and restitution.

With $6 million in the bank, you might think Frank would decide to draft an estate plan and decide who would get his money if he should suddenly die. Well, he did seek legal counsel after some cajoling from a friend, and a plan was hammered out—but Frank decided to put off implementing the plan until after he returned from a scuba-diving vacation.

Unfortunately, Frank died while on his vacation. His heart gave out during a scuba outing. So what happened to Frank's millions? Without a plan of his own, the state was put in charge of doling out his assets. According to the laws of Frank's state, his money would go to his closest living heir, who was his father. For many of us, that would be a fine solution. But Frank's father was a broken man with several million dollars in legal judgments against him. Between the judgments and the estate taxes, Frank's entire estate was about to disappear into the pockets of strangers.

The estate was saved when Frank's father wisely agreed to "disclaim" the inheritance. In other words, he simply said, "No, I don't want it," and it passed on to the next eligible heir: Frank's sister. The plan went through without a hitch, but another fight ensued when Frank's father accused his daughter of not caring for him the way she should have after having received Frank's money. The situation was eventually resolved, but not without a good dose of heartache and bickering, all of which could have been avoided had Frank simply signed his will before he left on his last vacation.

Each state has its own distribution rules for an intestate estate, or one without a will. The process is pretty similar throughout the country, however. Often, the surviving spouse gets everything, especially if there are minor children involved. Some states will divide the assets between the spouse and the children, with the spouse getting one-third and the children inheriting the remaining two-thirds, for example. If there is no spouse and no children, as in Frank's case, the parents generally get everything. In the absence of parents, the siblings would most likely divide the assets, and so on. If the state cannot find any living heirs, it will take possession of the money and property.

Translation: If you don't plan, you let the state decide who gets your money. It won't care whether you dislike your sister, Susie. If she's your closest kin, she will benefit from your lifetime of hard work.

DICTIONARY

Intestate: A situation in which a person has died without a will.

Intestate succession: The legal distribution process that occurs when someone dies without a will.

OTHER PITFALLS OF NOT PLANNING

You may agree with your state's succession laws, and that would make sense. Most states try to draft their rules to represent what the average person would want. Generally speaking, most married couples would want their spouse and young children to have first dibs. Most single people, meanwhile, probably want their parents to benefit first, followed by their siblings.

Even if you agree with your state's succession plan, however, you should not leave these decisions to the state. This tactic can result in a number of other not-so-obvious problems that could have been controlled with proper planning.

Here are some of the commonly ignored pitfalls of state control:

- *Your teenage children are rolling in dough:* If the state leaves your assets to minor children, it's theirs to spend as they please once they reach the legal age of majority—generally eighteen years old. You may have wanted Junior to spend his inheritance on college, but the state won't stop him from spending it on fast cars and trendy nightclubs (or worse) if he so chooses.

- *The family heirlooms are callously divided:* The state doesn't care that you promised your little sister she could have Mother's coveted pearl necklace if you die. Personal belongings will be divided in the same manner as the other assets: The spouse gets first dibs, then the children. If heirs fight over your belongings, the state could order that everything be sold and the family divide the profits, in which case sentimental value takes a backseat to monetary value and that priceless pearl necklace is just another dollar figure.

- *The tax bill is as high as it could be:* The state doesn't care about minimizing estate taxes—and for good reason: Death taxes go straight to the state coffers. If you are lucky

8

enough to have a lot of money, your heirs can pretty much be sure that they'll see the maximum possible tax rate levied against the estate.

• *Your beloved pet is left homeless:* Pets are legally considered property and, therefore, dealt with in the same way as property. Whoever gets control of your companion animal can do with it as he or she pleases, including sending Fluffy to the pound where she may be put to sleep.

• *Your family is left penniless:* By not planning, you also risk leaving your family in financial trouble. Estate planning isn't just about dividing your property. It's also about making sure you leave your family members with the financial support they may need in your absence. You may not have enough money to ensure your family's lifestyle if you die. Planning gives you the opportunity to tally your assets—including debts—and determine whether your family's financial needs could be met if you died tomorrow. (And if not, you may need to consider life insurance to fill in the gaps.) People with young children often find that they don't have enough to provide for their kids, especially if that equation involves college tuition.

• *The new spouse gets all your money:* If your spouse remarries, your replacement spouse may have free rein to spend the inheritance as he or she pleases. If your former spouse dies before your replacement dies, your assets could become part of his or her estate. In other words, you and your former spouse's intended beneficiaries (meaning the people you actually want to get your stuff, like your kids) could get nothing.

• *Probate costs more:* Dying without a will can result in a more costly probate process, because it can create barriers to simpler probate proceedings. (Probate is the court-supervised process intended to ensure that your wishes are carried out when there's a legal will, and that your estate is handled according to state law if there isn't a will.) Formal probate is more expensive because, as one lawyer put it, you can't sneeze without permission from the court. (See chapter 9 for more information.)

Appointing a Guardian for Your Minor Children

Perhaps even more important than deciding who gets what from your property is deciding who gets to take care of your minor children if you die. If you don't name someone to raise your young children, the state will do it for you.

The person who gets the job may not be the person you wanted. Furthermore, you risk opening the door to nasty custody battles. Relatives from both sides could present equally compelling cases as to why they should be granted custody. It would be up to a judge to listen to the various cases and decide who'd be best suited to raise your family.

Hopefully, it won't come to this. And it usually doesn't. When one parent dies, the other parent will generally take over. But what if both parents die simultaneously? It's rare, but it does happen. That's not all. You need to plan for an alternate caretaker if you're the only living parent, or if the other parent is alive but unfit to take care of your children. (See chapter 3 for more information.)

No matter your situation, you should not delay drafting a will and naming a third-party person to be your children's guardian. The guardian will act as their new parent, feeding them and putting a roof over their heads until they're legal adults. You should also name a custodian (or trustee) to manage the children's inheritance and monitor their spending. (The guardian and the custodian can be the same person, but there are a lot of good reasons to name them separately. I'll get to that later.)

CHAPTER 2

INTRODUCING THE WILL

THE CENTERPIECE OF ANY ESTATE PLAN

No matter how little you know about estate planning, you probably have a good idea what a will is. A will is a legal document that you write during your life to explain who gets what when you leave this earth. It can also include instructions on other important after-death matters, such as the naming of someone to act as the guardian of your minor children.

Technically, a will is known as your Last Will and Testament. Under old common law, people would draft a document called a Testament that disposed of their real estate property. A separate portion of the document, called a Will, would dispose of all their personal property. Thus, the term *Last Will and Testament* still appears at the top of all will documents.

THE COMPONENTS OF A WILL

There are four main components to a will:

• *Naming the executor:* You get to name someone you trust to take charge of carrying out your wishes, as outlined in your will. This process is known as settling the estate, and this person is known as the executor—or personal representative in some states. He or she is responsible for making sure your stuff gets into the right hands when you die. It's not as simple, however, as calling a meeting of your heirs and telling them to make sure they take what's theirs on the way out. The executor has to settle the will through an established process known as probate, which can take anywhere from a few months to more than a year to complete. To put it bluntly, there's paperwork involved—a lot of paperwork.

• *Naming a guardian for your children:* The will is generally the only legal means you have for naming someone to take care of your children when you die. Keep in mind, however, that it's a nomination, not a guarantee. When it comes to minor children, the state has ultimate control. It's highly unlikely, however, that your wishes will be overridden. Courts tend to reject a deceased's choice of guardian only with serious cause, such as drug addiction, a troubling criminal history, or concerns that the environment could be abusive. (For more information on choosing a guardian, see chapter 3.)

• *Making bequests:* This is the part that everyone knows. The will allows you to name the people you want to inherit your property and possessions. For many people, this can be accomplished in a few lines. You might say, for example, "I leave $5,000 to the Marin Humane Society. Everything else will go to my husband, Bill. If he dies before me, my property and possessions will be divided equally between my two sisters, June and Jill." Generally speaking, while you can leave your property to whomever you want, there are some legal restrictions guiding who can be cut out of a will. Your spouse, for example, may have legal rights to some of your money. (See chapters 5 and 6 for more information.)

• *Establishing a trust:* A trust that's created through a will is known as a testamentary trust. You can use a will to create a trust when you die that will control your heirs' inheritances. (See chapter 10 for more information on testamentary trusts.)

DICTIONARY

Testator: The person who has written the will.

Beneficiary: Any person or entity (a charity, for example) that receives or is to receive assets, income, or property from an estate. This might be through a will, a trust, an insurance policy, or another distribution vehicle.

Heir: A person who acquires assets or property upon the death of another person based on the rules of descent and distribution. The term has also come to mean someone who receives or is expected to receive assets, income, or property from a will or trust.

NOTE: In this book, the terms *heir* and *beneficiary* are used interchangeably.

While most people know what a will is, you may still have a lot of questions about how wills work, including: *What makes a will legally binding? Do I need a lawyer to draft it or can I do it on my own? Does a will have to be typed or can it be handwritten? What are the limitations of a will, if any? Can I leave whatever I want to anyone I want or are there restrictions on my after-death transfers? Are the wishes outlined in a will enforceable? Who enforces them?*

Let's take a look at some of these questions more closely.

What Makes a Will Legally Binding?

There are some formalities required to make a will legal. Every state has different rules, however, so it's important to be up-to-date with your state's rules on writing a valid will. Here are some typical guidelines:

- *You must be of legal age and "of sound mind":* In order to draft a will, you need to be a legal adult, which generally means at least eighteen years old. You also need to be of sound mind. The legal requirements for this are fuzzy. Generally speaking, to have a sound mind you've got to know who your legal heirs are, and what you own.

- *The document should be typed:* Some states allow *holographic* wills, or wills that are handwritten. (Some even accept oral wills.) Most states, however, require that the document be typed. It's safest to type your will, since this is acceptable in all states whereas a holographic or oral will may not be. Whether you type or write your will by hand, you want it to be consistent throughout. A will that's half handwritten and half typed will create problems, even if the state normally accepts both types.

- *You must state that this is your will:* You want to clearly state that this is your will. Otherwise, it could be argued that it's just a piece of paper stating your wishes, but not legally a will.

- *You must make a bequest:* In order to make the will legal, you want to make a bequest or name someone to be guardian of your minor children. A document that says it's your will cannot be valid if it serves no purpose.

- *You must have witnesses:* After drafting your will, you want to sign and date it. Before you do this, however, you need to gather witnesses to review the signing process. Most states require just two witnesses, but some require three—so, just to be safe, three's a good number. All your witnesses should be present at the same time to witness your signing. You cannot have one witness present at the actual signing and another at a later date. After they witness your signature, your witnesses will also sign the will.

• *Witnesses cannot be beneficiaries:* Your witnesses cannot benefit from your will. You want a totally disinterested party, such as a neighbor or the receptionist in your office. Also, your witnesses should be legal adults, so don't rely on your twelve-year-old nephew.

In the majority of states, you can take an extra step to give your will a final seal of approval—thus saving a lot of hassle for your executor and witnesses down the road. To do this, you need what's known as a self-proving affidavit. If you don't know what this is, don't worry; your notary public should know and should be able to provide you with the proper forms. Once you get a notary public and the proper forms in place, you and your two or three witnesses sign the self-proving affidavit before the notary public. Such affidavits generally ask you to agree that you're of legal age to draft a will, that you're of sound mind, and so forth. It is strongly recommended that you complete the self-proving affidavit if your state permits it. Otherwise, one or more of your witnesses could be required to appear before a court to attest to the validity of the document, making an already difficult situation harder.

Do I Need a Professional to Draft a Will?

No. You can draft a will on your own without the help of a lawyer. So long as you follow the rules required to draft a valid will, it will be legally binding.

ARE THERE ANY RESTRICTIONS ABOUT WHAT I CAN TRANSFER WITH A WILL?

Yes. Not all property can be transferred with a will. Some assets, known as non-probate property, need to be passed down by other means. Most often, these are items for which you've already named a beneficiary should you pass away. The individual retirement account (IRA) is a prime example. When you open an IRA, you sign what's known as a beneficiary designation form. This form—not your will—determines who gets the assets in the account when you die.

You want a good understanding of how non-probate assets work when you create your estate plan. Otherwise, you risk creating problems for your heirs when you die. Say, for example, that you invest in several certificates of deposit (CDs) worth about $35,000. At the time you open the CDs, you decide to name your son Coleman the beneficiary—through a form provided by the bank—because he's the only one of your children who is a legal adult. Several years later, after all your children have left home, you go see a lawyer and draft a will requesting that all your assets be divided evenly among your three children, Colette, Coleman, and Chris. When you die, all your probate property will be divided evenly as you requested. The CDs, however, will be given to Coleman. He doesn't have to divide them among his siblings, regardless of your wishes that all your assets be equally divided. According to the distribution rules that govern the CDs, that money is his to keep. (For more information on the importance of updating beneficiaries for non-probate assets, see chapter 5.)

Here's a list of property that lies beyond the purview of the will, also known as non-probate property:

- *Joint tenancy property:* If you own property (real estate deed, bank account, car title, and so on) in joint tenancy, you're giving the other owner (or owners) permission to take over your share when you die. This is known as a right of survivorship.

- *Beneficiary designation property:* Property or assets that require you to sign a beneficiary designation form are also beyond the purview of a will. This generally includes life insurance policies and most tax-sheltered retirement accounts, such as the 401(k) and the IRA. When you die, the beneficiary designation form—not the will—will direct who gets the assets.

- *Payable-on-death accounts:* This works much like the beneficiary designation form, except for bank accounts including CDs. You simply fill out a payable-on-death form naming a beneficiary. The beneficiary has no control over the account until you die. When you die, the beneficiary can have access to the money in the account after proving your death and his or her beneficiary status.

- *Transfer-on-death accounts:* Some brokerage accounts allow you to open a transfer-on-death (TOD) account, which allows you to name someone to take over your account when you die. Not all states allow this, however. To find out if your state allows TOD accounts, go to the Web site of the National Conference of Commissioners on Uniform State Laws (www.nccusl.org).

- *Living trust property:* A living trust is often viewed as a will substitute because whatever assets you transfer to the trust during your life are automatically transferred to the named beneficiary when you die. Indeed, much like a will, the trust document directs distribution of property upon death.

Be careful not to confuse joint tenancy with tenancy in common, which requires the property to be probated. If Bill buys a house with his friend Fred, and titles it as joint tenancy property, Bill's share will automatically go to Fred when he dies. Likewise, Fred's property will be left to Bill. It doesn't matter if a will is uncovered that says differently. If Bill and Fred own the property as tenancy in common, on the other hand, they are reserving their right to leave their respective shares to whomever they want when they die. If you want to avoid probate and leave your share to your co-owner when you die, make sure you title the property as joint tenancy property. Married couples would use tenancy by the entirety, which operates in much the same way.

Misunderstandings about the difference between joint tenancy and tenancy in common can cause a lot of problems after death. Consider Thomas's story. He was a young man who had just bought a house with his fiancée, Terry. Shortly after his death, Terry discovered that she owned only half of the house through tenancy in common. Since Thomas didn't have a will, and the couple wasn't yet married, Thomas's half of the house went to his closest living relatives: his parents. Terry thought the house should be hers, but Thomas's parents decided to keep their inherited share. As a result, Terry refused to let go of some of the personal effects that Thomas's parents wanted to remember him by, a battle that went on for several months, adding stress to an already difficult situation.

It's impossible to know what Thomas's intentions were regarding the house. He may have been confused about the difference between joint tenancy and tenancy in common, or he may have wanted to leave his half of the house to his parents. Regardless of his intentions, Terry was clearly confused about the difference between the two types of ownership—and that was enough to trigger problems following Thomas's death.

When dividing non-probate property, you also want to consider the impact your debts might have on who gets what. Your debts will be taken from your probate property first. So if you divide your assets without this fact in mind, you might end up unintentionally giving unequal distributions. Suppose you want to divide your property equally between your son and daughter and you decide to leave your son your IRA, which is worth $100,000. To even things out, you give your daughter your non-retirement brokerage assets, which are also worth $100,000. Since all debts are paid from your *probated* property, however, the payments will first come out of your daughter's share, leaving her with less than her brother.

CAN I LEAVE MY MONEY TO WHOMEVER I WANT?

Yes and no. You can leave your money to whomever you want—including a group of perfect strangers—as long as you don't cut off certain people in the process. There are rules protecting spouses—and sometimes children—from being disinherited. Know the rules of your state before you disinherit either of these groups.

WHO WILL ENFORCE MY WILL WHEN I DIE?

Now that you know what it takes to draft a legally binding will, it's important that you feel confident your efforts will pay off. One of the main benefits of drafting a will is that you get to name the person you want to enforce your wishes when you die. Legally speaking, this person is called the executor or the personal representative. When someone agrees to be your executor, that person has basically agreed to carry out certain responsibilities for you when you die. He or she will be responsible for protecting your property until it can be distributed to your rightful heirs; for making sure all your debts are paid; for filing your tax returns; and, of course, for distributing your property and assets.

If you don't name your own executor, the state will do it for you. If no one you trust comes forward to claim this responsibility—

or the court decides that those willing to do the job aren't a good fit—a court-appointed attorney will usually be named. This may cost your estate more money than naming your own executor.

Behind the technical term *executor* is usually a mourning spouse, a trusted sibling, or a devoted child. As such, people often wonder: *How will my executor know what is required to settle the estate?* Well, the executor will follow certain pre-established procedures required to settle the estate. A local court, known as the probate court, will be there to guide and enforce the rules. Also, in addition to being personally bound to you and your trust, the executor is legally bound to preserve your estate and not waste or steal money from it.

If your executor feels overwhelmed, he or she can always hire a lawyer or other professional to help with the process. He or she might also consider buying or borrowing a guidebook for executors at the local bookstore or library. Indeed, you might want to consider providing your executor with just such a book to help manage the job.

> **LOOK OUT!** Before you draft your will, you want to consider whether or not you should use another wealth transfer tool, such as a living trust. The main benefit of the living trust is that it allows your executor to avoid probate. (For more information about living trusts, see chapter 8.)

CHAPTER 3

PLANNING FOR MINOR CHILDREN

FINDING A GUARDIAN THEY WILL RESPECT

A lot of people who would otherwise never plan for their deaths are inspired to write a will because they worry about what might happen to their young children if they die. It's common for young parents to draft a will right before flying off together on their first vacation without the kids. Sometime between buying the plane tickets and hiring the babysitter, they wonder: *What if the plane crashes and we both die? Who will take care of the kids?*

If you have minor children (any child not yet a legal adult), your estate planning concerns are probably more focused on providing for them than on distributing your assets or lessening your potential estate tax bill. Certainly, it's an important goal—although not an easy one to contend with.

If you have one or more minor children, you want to consider three things:

- Who will take care of your children if you die?

- Who will provide for them financially?
- Who will manage the money you leave for them?

CHOOSING A GUARDIAN

The first step in planning for your children is to find someone who will take care of them if both parents die. This person, in legal terms, is known as the guardian.

If just one parent dies, the other parent will generally retain control of the children. It doesn't matter if you're separated, divorced, or were never married. The surviving parent will get control of the children unless there are serious concerns about that parent's ability, which would require proof of problems such as neglect, drug abuse, or a criminal record.

Most states will allow you to name a guardian only through a will, not through any other means, including a living trust. You should examine the rules of your state before proceeding. Regardless, it would be wise to draft a will for this purpose just in case you move.

Finding a guardian is often the toughest part of estate planning. You will never find the perfect replacement for you and your spouse. Still, you want to be selective. Here are some factors that can help you choose the most qualified person for the job:

- *Is your choice physically able to handle the job?* "Mom and Dad are the perfect choice. After all, they raised me, and I turned out all right. I want my kids to grow up with the same values and lessons I learned as a child." If this sentiment is true for you, wait a second before you ask Mom and Dad if it's okay to name them guardians of your children. Consider, first, whether they're physically capable of carrying out the tasks required. Even if they're healthy and spry now, they may not be able to continue the job as your children age.

- *Will your kids maintain the same lifestyle?* Your sister Annie is the best choice. She loves the kids and would raise them in a fashion similar to your own. Your husband and your kids agree. But Annie lives in Texas and you've raised your kids in Vermont. Your kids would be uprooted from their childhood home. They would have to change schools and make new friends. Is it worth it?

- *Does the guardian share your moral and religious beliefs?* Your brother is a fabulous husband and father, and he would do a great job raising your kids. He's an atheist, however, and you and your wife firmly believe in attending weekly religious services as a family. Would your brother raise your kids with your religious and moral beliefs, such as attending weekly religious services, if he were their guardian?

- *You've picked a fabulous couple. Great. What if they divorce?* It's better not to pick couples as guardians in case they divorce or split up. If your sister Annie is the main person you want to be guardian, nominate her. Don't nominate "Annie and her husband, Todd," no matter how great a father you think he would be.

- *What would your children want?* It's important that your children respect your choice. They don't have to love or cherish the new guardian, as those feelings take time to develop, but they should respect and generally like that person. You would want their new home life to run as smoothly as possible, for the children's sake and the guardian's as well. If the children respect the guardian, this is more likely to happen.

Once you've homed in on a name, you need to clear your decision with that person. This can be hard, but you have to do it.

The best approach is to be direct. Let him or her know what you want and why. Be sure to offer time to think about it. It's not a decision to be made on the spot.

Keeping the name of the chosen guardian secret until after death can make for good movie and television dramas, but it's not a smart thing to do. The movie *Raising Helen** is a perfect example. A young modeling agency assistant is totally surprised by her dead sister's request that she raise her orphaned nieces and nephews. (Helen is the party sister who leaves family functions early to attend fancy Manhattan parties with her model friends.) When Helen learns of her sister's decision (in a lawyer's office), she isn't totally sure she wants the responsibility. When she finally decides to accept her dead sister's wishes, she's totally unprepared. She has to change her entire life, uprooting the kids, enrolling them in a new school—and even giving them up at one point in the movie before, once and for all, deciding that she can handle the job.

This isn't to say that a guardian who knows ahead of time that he or she has the job will be without problems. Anyone who's given the task of suddenly caring for someone else's children would have to make some adjustments. But the guardian should at least be mentallly prepared.

Even when your guardian agrees to do the job, you want to get an update every few years. People's lives change, and the idea of taking care of someone else's kids, while doable at one point in life, can seem an impossible burden at another. Keep an eye out for big lifestyle changes—a terminally sick child, the loss of a job, a divorce. Dramatic shifts in responsibility, income, and personal stability can lessen the chances that your choice will want to step in and take over your children's care if you die to-

---

Raising Helen, directed by Garry Marshall and starring Kate Hudson and John Corbett. Released in 2004 by Walt Disney Pictures.

morrow. You and your spouse will want to consider how such changes in your guardian's life could affect your decision, even if the guardian's commitment isn't affected. A move to a new state, in addition, could lead you to seek out a new guardian who is committed to the community in which you live. A divorce might also spur you to seek out a new caretaker.

In addition to your top choice, you want to name one or two successor guardians. This is very important to guard against the possibility that your named guardian can't serve when the time comes. Say, for example, that you name your sister Susie, who dies in the same accident that takes your life. Had you named your best friend, Henry, successor guardian, he could take over. The saying in the legal community is, "Better your second choice than some judge's first choice."

Your Choice Isn't Guaranteed

Naming someone guardian in your will doesn't guarantee he or she will get the job. The final decision rests with the courts. Children aren't property and, therefore, cannot be willed away like a car or a house. Also, the guardian can change his or her mind. Or another person may oppose your decision. The state can reject your choice, opposed or unopposed, for several reasons:

- The guardian is deemed unfit for the job.
- The guardian is dead or severely ill.
- The guardian rejects the appointment.

It's highly unlikely, however, that your wishes will be overridden. Courts tend to reject the deceased's choice of guardian, if both able and willing, only with serious cause.

Dealing with an Ex-Spouse

What do you do if you don't want your children's other parent to have control of the kids if you die and he or she survives? Maybe your ex-wife is a bad parent. You think that your new wife will make a better mother. After all, she's been caring for them like they were her own since you two married.

No matter what your reason, it's not your choice to make. If one natural parent is still alive, he or she will be considered the guardian. You cannot cut off your ex-spouse's rights to be the parent simply by naming someone else the guardian in your will.

You can, however, try to get the court to reject your ex as the guardian. Generally, that means showing the court that your ex-spouse has either abandoned the children, or that he or she is unfit to be a parent. To show someone is unfit, you usually have to demonstrate serious problems such as drug abuse, mental illness, or criminal activity.

WHO WILL PROVIDE FOR THEM FINANCIALLY? UNDERSTANDING LIFE INSURANCE

The next question you need to ask yourself is: *Who will provide for my kids financially?* Well, hopefully, you will. What's the point of choosing the perfect guardian to care for your kids if that person never has time for them because he or she has to work extra jobs to pay for their needs? The last thing you want is for your children's guardian to have to move to a smaller home, scrimp on groceries, or plain refuse to accept the position because you failed to plan financially.

People with young children and not a lot of assets have the perfect solution: life insurance. If you have young children, you want to seriously consider taking out a term life insurance policy to provide them with money to live on when you die. Again, a simple term policy is sufficient for the majority of parents. Term is generally quite inexpensive, yet it will cover your basic need—money to care for your children if you die before they are grown.

TECH TALK: Proceeds from life insurance policies you own will be counted as part of your taxable estate. Before buying a life insurance policy, you want to consider how it might affect your tax situation when you die. (See chapter 14 for more information.)

Term is so named because the policyholder pays money, or premiums, to the insurance company to be insured for a specified period of time, or term. You select the time period and the ultimate payout amount. If you die within that window, your beneficiaries will be paid the amount you have selected, which is known as the face value of the policy. Say your kids are four and six years old. You might get a term policy that covers your death for twenty years, at which time the younger would be twenty-four years old, out of college, and (hopefully) independent and earning a living. So long as you pay your premiums over that time period, your death will trigger a lump-sum payment to your beneficiaries for the next twenty years. If you survive the term, your policy will end and your kids will get nothing.

What About Permanent Life Insurance?

When shopping for life insurance, you are bound to run into a salesperson who wants to sell you a permanent policy. There are many variations on permanent insurance; the two main types are whole life and universal life. If an agent recommends permanent life insurance, it may be because you'd be better off with it. Keep in mind, however, that the sales pressure may also be born out of personal financial desires. Permanent life insurance policies come with much better commissions for the salesperson than do term policies. Unscrupulous salespeople will try to sell them to anyone, regardless of need.

A general rule of thumb to consider is that most people don't need permanent life insurance. There are, however, a few exceptions.

First, an explanation of how permanent life insurance differs from term insurance. Permanent life insurance can cover you for life rather than just for a set period of time. It also comes with a savings account known as the cash value. You tap into the savings account portion of the policy by cashing in the policy or by borrowing against your death benefit. This may sound better than term insurance so far, but there are trade-offs. Prime among them is that you would pay a lot more in premiums and sales commissions for permanent insurance than you would for a plain-vanilla term policy. Also, the fees required to keep the policy in force can increase substantially as you age.

So who might want a permanent policy over a plain-vanilla term policy? The answer is: people who need coverage for life. This may include people who need insurance to pay off big debts or estate taxes when they die. It can also include people who need money to fund a trust for a child with special needs or disabilities, or another lifelong dependent. If you need insurance coverage for life, you should not rely on term insurance. Sure, you can hope to be re-insured after the policy ends, but this is a risky strategy. The insurance company may reject you or, at the very least, force you to pay substantially higher premiums as you age because the risk of a payout due to your death becomes more likely.

If you're considering a permanent policy, the main question you want to ask yourself is: *Why might I need a policy that protects against my death once my kids are grown?* If you don't know why you might need this, don't get it. If you have expenses that need to be covered and cannot be paid for with your present property or assets no matter when you die, you want to consider permanent life insurance. Likewise, you will want this type of insurance if you have lifelong dependents.

Certainly, don't be sold on the savings portion of permanent insurance. It's a good safety net for people who need lifetime insurance because it allows them to back out with some money if plans change. It's not a reason to buy this insurance, however. You can probably save just as well, if not better, by buying a term policy and placing the extra money you would have spent on a permanent policy in a savings account.

If you're torn, get a second opinion from a fee-only insurance analyst. These are professionals who, for a flat or hourly fee, will analyze your prospective plan and tell you the pros and cons of the pitch. These fee-only analysts aren't cheap, but buying a policy that you don't need will probably cost you more in the long run. Also, consider buying a term policy that can be converted into a permanent policy down the road if you think you might want this option available to you later.

When comparing term and permanent life insurance, some people will lean toward the permanent because they don't like the idea of their premiums going to waste. They might say, "Well, if I don't die within that time period, I have essentially lost my money." If you're thinking this way, you're missing the point. That's like saying people should total their cars in order to benefit from their car insurance. Insurance is there to protect against something you hope won't happen. If you need insurance for a very long time, you want permanent insurance. If not, go for term. If you don't die before that period is up, be grateful.

TECH TALK: A special feature of certain permanent life insurance polices is that you can use your savings account, or cash value, to fund your policy premiums. Sales agents often sell this feature as a way to maintain a policy without having to pay premiums as the cash value grows. In order for that to happen, however, your cash value needs to actually rise. The technology-stock bust in 2000 meant that a lot of policies investing in the tech market ended up with negative cash values. Some policyholders had to pay more in premiums than they'd expected—or risk losing some of their coverage.

How Much Life Insurance Do I Need?

This is a critical question to ask yourself when buying insurance. There are two main methods for determining how much insurance you'll need. The first is the income method: Take your current annual earnings and multiply them by seven. If you make $50,000 a year, for example, you would want coverage of $350,000. Be sure to include the price of important employee benefits, such as health insurance. The second method involves determining your spending needs. To do this, calculate recurring costs, such as mortgage payments, health insurance, private schooling, child care, and monthly living expenses, and combine this figure with other important expenditures, like college. This method can be useful when calculating insurance coverage for a stay-at-home spouse who doesn't have an income. With one partner at home, the family dramatically reduces many costs, including child care, laundry, and housekeeping. If that spouse were to die, these services would have to be provided by people who charge money. Insurance can help pay these expenses. You also want to include the short-term costs that will come with your death, such as a funeral and any lawyer's fees involved in closing the estate. Also, consider how insurance can help alleviate any debts that might be owed by your estate when you die.

Finally, as you calculate how much life insurance you need, be sure to consider the value of whatever assets and property you are planning to leave to your spouse or children when you die. This includes any income sources that might still be available after your death, such as Social Security or a company pension. In other words, be careful about buying too much insurance.

WHO WILL MANAGE THE MONEY I LEAVE THEM? FINDING A CUSTODIAN

In addition to making sure you have enough money to provide for your kids if you die, you also want to strategize ways to get that money into their hands. You can leave the money to your kids directly, but this method has some drawbacks.

For one thing, if your children are too young to manage the inheritance themselves, the court will appoint someone to do it for them. The appointed person—known as a custodian, property guardian, or property manager—is often the caretaker guardian, but not always. In other words, the judge has the power to appoint an outside lawyer to control the child's inheritance. That could cost your child some money, since a court-supervised custodian is entitled to fees from the minor's estate.

Also, your children will inherit any funds remaining in the estate when they become legal adults, generally at age eighteen. This may or may not be what you want to happen. If you're like most parents, you don't want your kids to inherit large amounts of money at such a young age.

If you prefer to institute controls over their inheritance, you have to do it in your estate plan. There are several methods for implementing controls over the money you leave to your minor children:

- *Name a custodian or property guardian:* You can name your own custodian, or property manager, in your will. This person will still be closely monitored by the court. For some people, this might be perceived as a good thing. Generally speaking, though, it's a hassle for the custodian. When under court supervision, a custodian is required to submit yearly reports of all the transactions made with the child's inheritance. These reports are public files available for review by anyone who might want to check up on the property manager's spending. Plus, just as with a court-appointed custodian, the guardian can accept fees, which can dwindle the child's inheritance, and the child gets control of the assets when he or she reaches adulthood.

- *Set up a Uniform Transfers to Minors Act (UTMA) custodianship:* Passing money to a child under UTMA rules can often save your custodian a lot of hassle and allow you to extend the age at which your child gains control of the funds. UTMA is a set of rules that permit and govern powers of custodianship over wealth transfers made to minors. The rules say that you can give assets or property to a minor child and name a custodian to manage the money. This custodian also has broad powers to spend the money without court supervision. The custodian must, however, spend it for the benefit of the child or risk violating state laws. Some states require that money under UTMA custodianship be turned over to the child when he or she reaches legal adult age, which can be as young as eighteen. Others allow parents to extend the age at which the child can collect to as late as twenty-five. Check the rules of your state before relying on this benefit. Another potential drawback to this method is that not all states have adopted UTMA rules; again, check your own state's rules before you set one up.

• *Set up a pot trust:* This type of trust allows your trustee to spend money according to need. If one kid needs braces, the trust money can be withdrawn for that purpose. If another needs ballet lessons, money can be used for that. Funds are available for special schooling or special medical treatment as well. In other words, a pot trust allows the inheritance to be put in one pot and spent much the way a typical family would have spent it: as needs arise. The main drawback is that this can lead to certain inequities (also much like the typical family), and can place a good amount of burden on the trustee to decide what expenses are worthwhile. If one child could benefit from special medical care, well, it's quite obvious that the money should be used for that, even if it leaves less for the other kids. Other situations are less obvious, however. What if your oldest daughter, Samantha, is admitted to a very elite, but expensive, private high school? If the trustee agrees to pay for Samantha's high school tuition, there may not be enough to do the same for the other children when their time comes. Is she getting an unfair advantage because she's the oldest, or is the investment worth it because she worked hard to earn admission to this elite school? These are all highly idiosyncratic questions that need to be addressed as you plan.

• *Set up individual trusts:* You can also set up a trust for each child. With this method, the children each get an equal share and the trustee cannot spend more on one child than another. Generally, the trustee will be instructed to spend money for the child's health, education, and living expenses. When each child reaches a certain age—one that you can specify—the trustee will be instructed to end the trust and hand over whatever property remains to the beneficiary.

When deciding between a trust and a custodianship, you want to consider how much money you have to leave to your children. Generally speaking, people with a lot of money to leave behind want to rely on trusts because they can better control the age at which their children will ultimately inherit. People without a lot of money may prefer a custodianship, because setting up a trust can be pricey. Also, consider your children's ages. People with older children often turn to custodianship or individual trusts. Those with younger kids are more likely to rely on pot trusts because it's harder to know if one child might need more money than the others.

> **LOOK OUT!** Be careful not to name young children beneficiaries of large life insurance policies without setting up the proper protections to ensure that the money will be under the control of your appointed custodian or trustee when you die. That means talking to the insurance company about how to coordinate your insurance with your trust or UTMA custodianship. Generally, you can name a trust as beneficiary; life insurance proceeds will then fund the trust. Also, most insurance companies will work with you if you want to name a custodian under UTMA to manage the proceeds if collected while the beneficiaries are still minors.

Whom Do You Want to Be in Charge of the Children's Money?

Whether you choose a pot trust, an individual trust for each child, or UTMA custodial power, you need to decide whom you want to act as your children's custodian or trustee. In other words, you need to pick someone to be in charge of spending their money until they're old enough to take over.

Very often, the person named as guardian is also named custodian or trustee. It makes sense to give the person who has powers over feeding and clothing your children the power to control the money that's used to pay for all this stuff.

Sometimes, however, you'll want to consider a separate person for the job. It's possible, for example, that your guardian won't want the responsibility of both raising the kids *and* managing the money. It's also possible that your guardian, while a great caregiver, isn't the most responsible person financially. Before deciding on your custodian or trustee, here are some factors to consider:

- Would your custodian use the inheritance only for your child's benefit?
- Would your custodian be careful not to commingle your child's inheritance with his or her own funds?
- Would your custodian manage the funds well, being aware of expenses and wary of investment risk?
- Would your custodian know when to seek professional assistance?
- Would your custodian keep careful and accurate records of the spending?

What if a Child Is Born After You Created Your Estate Plan?

Many states have what are known as permitted heir statutes, which aim to protect against any child being disinherited simply because he or she was born after you drafted your will. Whether or not the permitted heir rules take effect, however, depends on how you design your estate plan and distribute your money. Generally speaking, permitted heir rules apply to wills but not to non-probate assets such as beneficiary designation forms or living trusts. So if you are dividing your estate through non-probate assets, you want to assess how a new addition to the family will affect that plan. Some forms will allow you to name "all children living at my death" to account for the yet unborn.

Whether a probate judge decides to give the accidentally disinherited child any money also depends on what you have left your other children. Generally, if you have no other children, the left-out child would get whatever he or she would have received (according to the laws of your state) had you died without a will. If you have other children but gave them nothing (say, you left everything to your spouse), the left-out child would get nothing, just like the other children. If, however, you left your other children an inheritance, the omitted child could be entitled to receive what he or she would have received had you given each child an equal share. If, for example, you left $100,000 in property and assets to your two children and a third was left out of the will, the court would probably give each child one-third of that $100,000, rather than $50,000 to each of the two children as you originally directed.

Adopted children are taken care of the same way. Probate courts make no distinction between adopted and birth children unless you specifically request it in your will. Stepchildren, on the other hand, are not considered your children by the probate court unless you have taken formal steps toward adoption. If you want a stepchild to inherit, it's best to specifically name that child in your will.

CHAPTER 4

THE IMPORTANCE OF CAREFUL DISTRIBUTIONS

UNEQUAL BEQUESTS MAY BE JUSTIFIED, BUT JILTED HEIRS WILL FIGHT BACK

If you're planning your estate and your children are grown, you have very different concerns from people with minor children. You're no longer worried about finding a guardian, but you are wondering how to divide your money between your kids. This chapter will help you understand some of the pitfalls you might encounter when dividing your assets and property among grown kids.

Anyone who has ever had kids knows how particular they can be about fairness. You can't give one child an ice-cream cone without giving something of equal value to the others. Even the perception of unfairness—a *slightly* larger slice of cake for Sis— can lead to squabbling and hard feelings.

Well, your kids may be adults now, but deep down they're probably still just as concerned about fairness. It's just that their concerns revolve less around cake and ice cream, and more around the money you gave Junior for college, or the car you bought for Sissy when she started working.

Problems can happen whether or not you're alive and available to act as judge and jury. Some arguments will remain discreet, while others will escalate into noisy, costly disputes. Some will be resolved with time, while others will cause lifelong divisions.

The whole question of splitting your estate may seem like an easy one if you just do what you did when they were kids and make sure everything is divided equally. When it comes to money, however, that is easier said than done. There are so many ways you can inadvertently give more to one heir, leaving the others feeling cheated or angry. You might, for example, give one child a loan that is never paid back. This may seem like a small deal to you—ancient history, in fact—but not to your other children, the ones who didn't benefit from an equally generous "loan."

There are also many ways in which you might justify—rightly or wrongly—why one child deserves more than the others. A daughter may have put her life on hold to take care of you when you were sick, while the others went on with their lives as usual. Or perhaps you feel one child needs it more because of a sickness or a change in career. If you are considering any of these tactics, however, you should also be asking yourself: *At what cost? Will an unequal distribution create divisions among my normally close children?*

GIVING SEPARATE ASSETS COULD CAUSE SERIOUS INEQUITIES

Your kids never really got along, so you don't want them to jointly own the family home when you die. At the same time, you don't want it sold simply because they can't agree on anything. You decide to leave the home to your daughter, who has expressed interest in living there with her family someday. So as not to cheat your son, you leave him stocks of equal value, which he will enjoy more anyway.

You die ten years later. Your son inherits the stocks and your daughter inherits the house. Many of the hot stocks you invested in, however, are now defunct. The value of your son's inheritance has been permanently halved. Meanwhile, a local real estate boom has increased your daughter's inheritance by 30 percent.

This can happen with similar assets as well. You may choose to leave your son shares of one company's stock, and your daughter shares of another company's. What happens when your son's company comes out with a new product and your daughter's company sends its president to jail? Again, the inheritance may be unequal.

It happened to the Schneiders, a loving couple who always treated their children fairly.

The Schneiders didn't have a lot of money, but they had two homes. So each child, a son and a daughter, was to get one of the homes when the last parent died.

As luck, bad luck, would have it, Mr. and Mrs. Schneider left this world sooner than they expected. One of the homes—the one that was to go to their daughter—still required regular mortgage payments. Needless to say, the daughter was upset that she was left with a debt-ridden gift, while her brother benefited from a problem-free inheritance.

The children eventually agreed to pay off the mortgage together, but not before a good amount of crying and squabbling.

Solution: Make Them Share

Dividing an inheritance by asset class can seem like a good idea on the surface: If they each get their own toy to play with, they won't fight. But this tactic carries too much risk.

If you own assets that can fluctuate in value, it's best to divide them among your children. This way they share any misfortunes that might come with the inheritance, including lawsuits, damage from natural disasters, or sudden worthlessness. They also equally benefit from any gain.

If they don't want to own it together, one child can buy the others out. The Schneiders, for instance, could have made the children co-owners of the houses and let them decide between themselves who would get which one. The one who took the house with the mortgage could then demand monetary compensation from his or her sibling.

If you're worried that they will waste time and money bickering over ownership of, say, a house, put the assets in a trust. Appoint a third-party trustee to watch over your children's interactions. The trustee may have instructions to initiate a sale of the asset if they can't come to an agreement. The children can then divide the proceeds.

Forgot About That "Loan" to Junior Twenty Years Ago? Nobody Else Has

There comes a point in every parent's life when a child asks for a good chunk of money that the parent doesn't want to give away. If it's for a good reason—to buy a house, to start a business, to pay the rent between jobs—it can also be hard for parents to say no.

To resolve the situation, many parents decide to treat the transaction as a loan. They tell the child that they expect to see every penny returned as soon as possible. The child will often eagerly agree to the terms, only to never honor them—or stop honoring them after just a few initial payments.

You should know, however, that ignoring these debts could hurt your heirs when you're gone.

Look at the Allison family. Mr. Allison had four daughters and one son. When he died, the sisters recounted stories their father had told them about the debt his one son owed him. According to these stories, the son asked for the money when he was moving across the country as a way to help him get started with his new life. Mr. Allison agreed to give his son the money, but on the condition that he repay it once he settled in his new home. Mr. Allison, the daughters said, never saw his son or his money again.

The sisters, believing their father's account 100 percent, decided that the debt should be deducted from their brother's share of the inheritance. When they confronted their brother about their plan, however, he rejected it. Why? The money was a gift, not a loan, he said.

The sisters were shocked. They assumed he would balk about repaying, but never suspected he would deny it was a loan. They quickly realized they had no proof to indicate that it was, indeed, a loan, and, therefore, little leverage to force repayment.

Solution: Put Everything in Writing

If you lend your children money, keep records of how much was loaned as well as any payments made on the debt. If you die without records of the debt, you leave your children susceptible to squabbles over how much is outstanding. Or, as happened with the Allison family, you leave your children arguing over whether there ever was any debt to begin with.

The best records will be the ones that come from formalizing the loan process. That means drafting a contract with terms for repaying the debt, and requiring that your child sign it. You want to charge interest and present the child with a timeline for when you expect payments to start. It helps to get other family members involved. The more people who know about the transaction, the more pressure there will be to pay it back. These actions help enforce the idea that the money must be repaid. You are saying, *I take this seriously.*

Still, there's never any guarantee. If you don't get your money back, make note of it in your will. You can ask that whatever debt remains upon your death be deducted from the indebted child's share of the inheritance.

This action alone could provide the incentive needed to get the loan repaid. Why? Well, the interest accumulated from the time you made the loan until the day you die could be enough to deplete that child's entire inheritance, depending on the interest rate and the length of your life. Point this out to the indebted child and use it as an opportunity to make a deal. Say, "If you pay off the principal now, I will forgive the interest due on the loan. Otherwise, it will all be deducted from your inheritance, including interest, when I die."

THE CHILD WHO NEEDS IT MOST DOESN'T NECESSARILY DESERVE IT

Your son has an alcohol addiction that he's been trying to shake. You plan to support him until he kicks the habit.

Your daughter is an aspiring artist and needs occasional help to pay the rent.

Your son works hard and has a good job. With five kids, though, he needs help putting them through college. You plan to give him more than his brother, who has a higher-paying job and just one child.

Your daughter has a learning disability that will prevent her from ever being completely independent. You need to put money away to protect her when you're gone.

Whatever the situation, parents often spend extra money on the child who needs it more. A recent academic study, "Why Parents Play Favorites: Explanations for Unequal Bequests,"* found

---

*"Why Parents Play Favorites: Explanations for Unequal Bequests," by Audrey Light, Department of Economics, The Ohio State University, and Kathleen McGarry, Department of Economics, University of California–Los Angeles, with financial support from the National Bureau of Economic Research. Published in 2002.

that among mothers who plan to bequeath to their children un-equally, as many as 33 percent will do so based on need. Of these, two-thirds refer to needs other than a disability, such as the fact that one child makes more than another.

Some needs, like a mental or physical disability, no doubt require extra financial support from the family. It would be shameful if one child were to argue otherwise for his or her own benefit. Providing extra financial support because one child makes more than the siblings, however, could be viewed as a preference rather than a necessity. The other children may resent it.

Solution: Keep It Equal—or at Least Talk About It

Before giving more to one child based on need, seriously consider whether that "need" is a real one in the eyes of your other children. Think of it this way: Could one child argue that you are simply helping the less successful rather than the more needy child? If so, you would be sending the message that failure generates more affection from Mom and Dad than success. It also helps encourage what may become an unbearable dependency on Mom and Dad.

Unless one child has a serious disability or illness, it's best to keep gifts among your children equal—both in life and in death. In other words, financial support for the needier child over a lifetime could be just as resented as an unequal inheritance. If you give rent money to the needy child, consider giving the other children an equal gift.

Of course, it's not always possible to give equally. If you can't afford to give everyone an equal gift, talk to the other children. Let them know what your plans are and that, while you would like to give to everyone equally, you cannot afford to do so.

Talking openly is very powerful. In this case, it will accomplish several things. It will prevent you from giving to the needy child too often, or for frivolous reasons. Since you have to talk to all your children every time you give to the needy one, you're more likely to limit your giving to the most critical situations. It will also send the message to your other children that you're not trying to reward failure, but simply to help someone in serious need. If it is, indeed, for a good reason, they will probably be sympathetic, and may even offer some support of their own. If it's not for a good reason, your kids will surely fight you on the gift.

Finally, consider giving to your grandchildren directly. Many times, help for the needier child can be met by providing assistance to the grandchildren. Say the needier child needs help paying the rent. You might say, "No, I can't keep giving you money to pay the rent, but I will take your children shopping for their school clothes." This alleviates at least one financial burden.

> **LOOK OUT!** Large financial gifts (over $12,000 per person per year) can trigger unwanted tax consequences, especially when it comes to gifts for grandchildren. (See chapter 14 for more information on how gifts can be taxable.)

Again, give equally. If you buy clothes or set up a college fund for one grandchild, you need to do the same for all the grandchildren. A word to the wise: Inequality among the grandchildren can cause far more bitterness in your children than inequality among siblings. It's one thing to hurt their feelings. You will have gone too far, however, if you hurt their children's feelings.

Should the Child Who Gives You More Get More?

All your children visit on a regular basis, but your son is the one who has sacrificed to take care of you. He drives you to all your appointments and cares for you when you're sick. He has already made it clear that if you ever become too frail to care for yourself, you can move in with him. Your other children, meanwhile, complain if you even ask them to do anything extra for you. So you don't ask anymore, and they prefer it that way.

Giving more to the child who gives you more is referred to as "the exchange motive": One child gives you more time, affection, or assistance, and in exchange, you give that child more money upon your death. As noted, about 33 percent of moms who plan to leave unequal bequests do so because of some type of exchange, according to the academic study mentioned above.

When we think of an exchange relationship, we tend to focus on physical care. But a parent may also want to give more to the child who has stuck around to work in the family business, or to the child who has always done what he or she was told. In other words, exchange-based giving can be for something as ephemeral as behavior.

Unlike need-based giving, exchange-based giving is often quite justifiable. It makes sense to reward the child who has spent time and energy caring for you when you're old and frail. It also makes sense to want to leave the family business to the child who has sacrificed to make it work. Financially rewarding children for behavior can be more difficult to justify. Moms and dads have been known to cut children out of their wills because they don't agree with their choice of mate, career, or religion—personal choices that arguably should not be tainted by a parent's money. Sometimes, though, the child's behavior may be egregious enough to warrant the financial consequences of being disinherited: The child may have a gambling problem or have committed a heinous crime.

The point is, the exchange method can often be justified. The problem is, even when it's totally logical, your other children may not see it that way. Children have been known to cry foul when it comes time to dole out the inheritance and the child who sacrificed everything for the parent has been given more. (Of course, there is always reason to suspect that one child may have taken over care in order to control the parent's final distributions. More about this in chapter 12.)

Consider Maria's story. Maria spent seven years taking care of her elderly aunt. Every day after work and on weekends she would visit her aunt and attend to her needs, staying later and later as her aunt grew frail.

As time went on, the aunt came to rely on Maria's care. She gave Maria power of attorney and made her executor of her will. At one point, she requested that Maria take her to an attorney so she could redraft her will and leave everything to Maria. At this, Maria protested. She could use the money, sure, but she didn't want to cut her siblings out. Although they didn't participate in their aunt's care to the same extent, they were also very close to her.

Instead, Maria accepted some of her aunt's valuable belongings, including her furniture and her jewelry. *Nobody will complain about such things,* she thought.

Maria was wrong. After her aunt died, her siblings did complain about the jewelry, and also about smaller items, including a refrigerator and some old records. The family fought, too, because Maria was chosen to be executor. Maria eventually divided many of the personal possessions her aunt had given her and peace was restored. "I didn't want to hear about it for the rest of my life," she said.

Solution: If You Can't Be Fair, Be Perfectly Clear

If you plan on giving more to the child who has given you more, you need to be perfectly clear about your intentions in your will and inheritance plan. Disputes often arise because the other siblings think the child who gets more is taking advantage of them or pulling the wool over their eyes—especially if that sibling was also named executor. It's common for siblings to believe that

Mom didn't really want to give Sister more, but Sister convinced her to cut her sons out. Indeed, undue influence is a legitimate problem. When an unequal inheritance is your choice, and not the result of undue influence, you need to protect your heirs against such suspicions. (See chapter 6 for more about protecting your heirs from will contests.)

You would also be wise to discuss these feelings with your children before you die. It's possible that the caretaker doesn't want to risk offending the other children, or that the other children, upon learning what it would take to get a fair share, will become more willing to step in and help.

Of course, coming clean can work against you. Lawyers often speak of cases in which the offended heirs have cut off ties with a parent for suggesting that an inheritance might be unequal. Still, it's better that these feelings are expressed now than when you are dead and the ostracized child is left with lots of money and no way to mend family ties.

By talking with your heirs, you might also be able to come up with a more agreeable solution. Perhaps you could give the family business to the child who worked for it if you agree to make the other children beneficiaries of a sizable life insurance policy. Or you might be able to agree that all the children will receive an equal inheritance, but the caretaker will get a small annual salary for expended time and effort.

CHAPTER 5

KNOW WHAT YOU OWN

WHAT IS YOUR ESTATE, ANYWAY?

A major part of estate planning is knowing what you own. After all, you can't give away what isn't yours to begin with. This means knowing what assets and property make up your *estate*—which is simply a legal term for your property and other belongings. Doing this isn't as simple as it might sound on the surface, however.

If you're single, the formula for tallying up your estate is simple and straightforward: It's the product of all your property minus your debts and liabilities. So long as you pay your debts, therefore, you have full rights to decide who gets what property when you die.

Married people, on the other hand, face a slightly more complex formula. In order to fully understand what you own, you need to understand the property ownership rules for married people in your state. It may seem logical to assume that you own everything that you paid for with your own money—but this isn't necessarily true. Even if your spouse never lifted a finger to help you pay for certain property, he or she may still have claim to part of that property when you die. And even if you provide richly for your spouse at your death, he or she may still have the right to claim certain property that you intended to leave to someone else.

To truly understand how this might happen, you want to understand the two different systems for classifying marital property: community property law and common law. Nine states—Arizona, California, Idaho, Louisiana, Nevada, New Mexico, Texas, Washington, and Wisconsin—recognize the community property system. All the other states, which represent the majority, recognize the common law property system. Alaska may also be considered a community property state, but the married couple must create a written agreement to put the community property rules into effect.

I Live in a Community Property State— What Do I Own?

Under the community property system, property acquired during marriage becomes joint property. Property acquired before the marriage or property received as a gift during the marriage is known as separate property. In other words, the car you bought before your marriage may be considered yours alone, as would the car you inherited from your uncle Hank during your marriage. If, however, you also bought a car during marriage, it will be considered part of the marital community property, even if it's titled under your name alone, because it was purchased with community property money. Half of it belongs to your spouse, and at your death, you can give away only your half of the car. If you fail to designate someone to take your half of the car at your death, your spouse may also get the right to your half, depending on the state.

Again, the only property considered separate is whatever you acquired prior to marriage or was gifted to you during your marriage, such as an inheritance. If you want separate property to remain separate, you must be careful not to commingle it with community property. This means that, for instance, the inheritance you received during marriage should remain in a separate account, not in your joint checking account. Otherwise, upon your death, the inheritance will likely be considered joint property, with half of it belonging to your spouse.

Rules regarding separate property can be more complex, depending on the state, so it's best to check your state's rules before deciding which property is separate and which is communal. Some states, for example, will treat income earned from separate property as community property, making it more difficult to ascertain who owns what.

I Live in a Common Law Property State— What Do I Own?

Under the common law system, property acquired during the marriage is your property to do with as you please at death, unless that property is titled as joint. Deciding who gets what when you die should, therefore, be relatively simple. Right?

Unfortunately, it's not so simple. While your property is yours, common law states tend to provide surviving spouses protections against being disinherited. These rules are generally referred to as the spousal elective share or spousal inheritance rights. This means that you can leave as much as you want to your spouse— from everything to nothing. A spouse who is displeased with his or her bequeathed share, however, can elect to claim his or her *legal* share. States generally allow the surviving spouse to claim an elective share of between one-third and one-half of assets. The spouse's inheritance rights may start off low and increase with the number of years married, depending on the state.

Let's assume, for example, that Ethan and Jessica have been

married for eight years. They live in a state with common law property rules. This state also permits an elective share of up to 50 percent of a spouse's inheritance.

Jessica was married previously, and she has two daughters from her first marriage. Ethan has not been married before and has no children. Ethan bought the house that they live in prior to his marriage to Jessica. It's titled in his name alone, but they both contribute to the expense of maintaining the house, including property taxes and mortgage payments. The house is worth about $300,000. Ethan also owns about $700,000 in retirement savings. Jessica, meanwhile, has roughly $250,000 in savings.

Let's first assume that Jessica pre-deceases Ethan, leaving all her money to her two daughters. If Jessica discussed her inheritance plan with Ethan beforehand, and he agreed to her decision, it's likely that everything will go as planned and Jessica's daughters will inherit $125,000 each. If Jessica's decision takes Ethan by surprise, on the other hand, he may choose to go against her wishes and claim his elective share, leaving Jessica's daughters with less. Technically speaking, he could claim as much as one-half of Jessica's property, or $125,000, leaving the daughters with $62,500 each instead of the $125,000 they expected.

If Ethan pre-deceases Jessica, the same rules would apply. If he leaves her in the cold, she could claim her elective share, or $500,000. Say Ethan leaves Jessica $500,000 in stocks and bonds from his IRA. He leaves everything else to his brother, including their house. Since Ethan has left Jessica half his estate, she has no right to renounce the will and claim her elective share. Her brother-in-law could ask her to leave the house, even though she helped pay for it. Technically, it's Ethan's property to do with as he pleases, since it's titled in his name.

What property is considered up for grabs when calculating an elective share varies by state. Some states impose the right on the entire estate. Others limit it to the probated estate, which means that money placed in a living trust might escape the right-of-election rules.

> **TECH TALK:** There are strict time limits associated with a spouse's right to claim a legal share of the estate. In New York, for example, the law requires the spouse to file for his or her right of election within six months after an executor to the estate has been appointed. This is because the estate cannot stay in limbo forever. It needs to be settled, and the court wants to know rather quickly who is making claims on what assets.

WHAT HAPPENS TO MY PROPERTY RIGHTS WHEN I MOVE?

From Common Law to Community Property

If you acquire an asset in a common law state and then move to a community property state, does it remain separate or become community property? The answer, unfortunately, depends on the state. California and Washington, for instance, would treat the property as community property, where each partner owned an equal interest. Other states would treat the property according to the laws of the state where it was acquired. In Texas and Arizona, for instance, separate property acquired in a common state would remain separate property.

From Community Property to Common Law

If you acquire property in a community property state and then move to a common law state, does property once deemed joint suddenly become separate? No. Property acquired in a community property state will generally be treated as joint property by the common law state.

How Else Can Marriage Impact Ownership?

The Impact of Nuptial Contracts

One way to get around the rules of your state is to create and sign a legal contract that outlines what each spouse owns and what his or her legal rights are when the other spouse dies. Such contracts, known as nuptial agreements, allow either party to waive rights given them by law. With a nuptial agreement, you can legally disinherit a spouse. So long as both parties voluntarily waive their inheritance rights, this is perfectly legal. Nuptial agreements can be signed before marriage (a pre-nuptial) or after marriage (a post-nuptial).

The Impact of Divorce

Every state reacts to divorce differently when it comes to estate plans. Some states terminate a former spouse's inheritance rights in the event of a divorce—the will is treated as if the former spouse had died. In other states, the entire will may be revoked due to a divorce. In others still, divorce has no effect on a will. Even if a state revokes inheritance rights under a will, it may not have the same power when it comes to living trusts. No matter what your state's laws, it's always a good idea to revise your estate plan after a divorce to make it clear if you want whatever assets were formerly bequeathed to the spouse to be bequeathed to someone else.

> **LOOK OUT!** If you are separated but not divorced, your spouse may still have the right to claim a certain portion of your assets. In order to cut him or her out of your will, you may need to show that the separation is leading toward a divorce, not just a little time off.

The Special Case of Non-Probate Assets

One potential benefit of a will is that it makes allowances for changes in your life. If you get divorced, get married, or have another kid, many states will take such changes into consideration even if you never change your will to reflect them. Non-probate assets, however, are an entirely different story. Even if your state has laws that allow non-probate assets to automatically reflect life changes, such as divorce, you don't want to rely on these laws to protect you. Why? Well, because many non-probate assets, like pensions, 401(k) plans, 403(b) plans, and employer-sponsored life insurance, aren't governed by the state. The Employee Retirement Income Security Act (ERISA) governs these assets because it governs employer-sponsored plans and benefits. ERISA is a federal law and, as such, it can supersede the rules of the state, allowing an ex-spouse to inherit your pension or 401(k) assets simply because you failed to change your beneficiary designation form.

Consider the case of David A. Egelhoff and Donna Rae Egelhoff,[*] which went all the way to the Supreme Court. David had named Donna the beneficiary of his employer-sponsored pension and life insurance policy while they were married. After four and a half years of marriage, however, the two separated and then divorced. A few months after the marriage was dissolved, David

---

[*]*Egelhoff v. Egelhoff* (99-1529) 532 U.S. 141 (2001).

died from injuries sustained in an automobile accident. The proceeds from the life insurance policy were paid to Donna. Despite agreeing to forgo rights to this pension in her divorce decree, she was also given rights to the pension assets due to ERISA rules that provide for the named beneficiary.

The children of David's first marriage disputed the distributions. On the surface, it would seem that their case had a lot going for it. For one thing, Donna had given up rights to the pension money as part of the divorce proceedings. Second, Washington State statute allowed that in the event of divorce, non-probate assets be distributed as if the former spouse had already died. It turned out, however, that ERISA is more powerful than the state, according to the U.S. Supreme Court, which decided that ERISA supersedes Washington State law and ruled in favor of Donna.

The point is: If you don't change your beneficiary designation forms, it doesn't matter what your will says, what a state statute says, or what a divorce decree says—you take a great risk that your money will be diverted to the wrong hands.

TECH TALK: When naming a beneficiary of any ERISA-governed assets, consider the rights of your spouse. A spouse has the right to claim all the money in plans such as a 401(k), 403(b), or other company-sponsored plans. If you want to leave the assets in that plan to someone else, you have to get your spouse's permission. Your company will probably require that he or she sign a waiver form to be filed with the human resource department.

Chapter 6

DISINHERITANCE

If You Must Cut Someone, at Least Cover Your Tracks

In the course of your planning, you might decide that you don't want to be fair in your distributions. Perhaps your son hasn't visited you in years, or your daughter has gone against your wishes and married someone you dislike.

That's fine. It's your money to do with as you please. Just be aware that cutting people out can be a dangerous game. Jilted heirs can try to grab a share by contesting the will in probate. They might claim that another heir—such as your new spouse—coerced you into cutting them out. They might suggest you were too old and muddleheaded to get it right, or claim the will was not properly drafted and, therefore, needs to be thrown out.

Even if the jilted heir doesn't win, the will contest can place an estate in limbo and deplete money from the rightful beneficiaries for legal fees. Heirs often settle with challengers just to end a tedious and costly fight.

STEP 1: KNOW YOUR LEGAL LIMITATIONS

The first step is to know what you own. Again, property that you think is yours may not be entirely so, depending on the rules of your state. As such, the first step to cutting someone out is to know what you own. (See chapter 5 for more information.)

Even when certain property *is* yours, you may be required to share some of it with specific people when you die. Thus, you need to know what death transfer rules control your distributions. Here's a basic rundown of the rules that may prohibit you from disinheriting certain people:

- **Spouse:** You can't disinherit a spouse unless he or she has abandoned you or has agreed to be disinherited in a legal contract. Most states have rules that protect the spouse from losing everything when the partner dies. Often a spouse is entitled to half of your property, or at least half of what you acquired during your marriage.

- **Children:** Most states do not provide children with automatic rights to your property. There are a few exceptions, however. In Florida, for example, the head of household must leave the residence to a spouse or child, if either one exists. Louisiana is also different from most states in that it has what are known as forced heirship rules. If you live in Louisiana, you will want to research these rules to know your rights. You may, for example, be required to leave a share of your estate to any child who has not yet turned twenty-four years old at the time you die. Grandchildren and children with permanent disabilities can also be forced heirs. Before disinheriting a child, it's best to review the rules of your state to make sure you are not breaking any laws and, thereby, creating a problem for your heirs when you die.

Step 2: Build Your Case

Once you have met the requirements of your state, it's your money to do with as you please. If you want to cut someone from your will, or divide your assets unequally, it's your right. Just cover your tracks.

Here are some tips to protecting your heirs and property from a jilted heir.

State Your Reasons

Unless the person you're cutting out is a child, you would simply not mention that person's name anywhere in the will or other documents. By not naming someone, you leave him or her nothing.

With children, the process can be a little trickier. Many states require that you specifically mention each of your children in your will. If you want to disinherit any of them, you should name them and then disinherit them. Even if you use a living trust, you should also have a will to make the disinheritance legal.

The bottom line is this: If you want to disinherit a child, it's best that you state clearly in your will that you are disinheriting this person and he or she gets nothing. Some attorneys suggest that clients write a letter to be attached to the will explaining why they chose to cut out the targeted heir. Even if you are disinheriting your child through a living trust or other means, be sure to go through this process. A disinherited child can still bring a lawsuit against a living trust.

Get It on Tape

Lawyers might also suggest that you videotape the will signing if you're worried about a will contest. You would need to hire a professional videographer and, in the presence of an attorney, explain why you chose to distribute your assets in this manner.

If you plan to videotape the signing, just be careful that you're not setting yourself up for another challenge. If you look confused or befuddled, the videotape could provide support for a case that you lacked testamentary capacity, which just means you weren't clearheaded enough to draft a legitimate will. In other words, the videotape technique can act as a double-edged sword. It can prove your intent and your capacity and put any will contests to bed, or—if you're not careful about what you say—it can be used against you in a court of law.

Add a No-Contest Clause

A no-contest clause is a legal instrument that can prevent heirs from fighting over what they get. It's a good technique to use when you're planning to give unequally. It essentially lets you say, *If you go against my wishes, you will be cut out.*

Say you want to give the family business to your daughter, who worked side by side with you over the last fifteen years. You aren't able to give your son an inheritance of equal value, but, being a fair person, you try to give him as much as you can. To protect against your son challenging your decision, you add in a no-contest clause. If he contests the will and loses, he loses his inheritance.

Remember: A no-contest clause needs to have "teeth." In other words, you need to leave your heirs enough to make them think twice about taking the risk that they might lose everything. A no-contest clause doesn't prohibit the heirs from challenging the will, or even from winning. It just means that if they challenge it and lose, they also stand to lose their share of the inheritance. If they challenge it and win, on the other hand, the no-contest clause fails along with the rest of the will.

So if you leave your son a measly $2,000 out of a $2 million estate, he's likely to toss the dice and contest the will. If he loses, he loses only $2,000, but if he wins, he stands to win a lot. Leave your son $100,000, on the other hand, and he will have more reason to accept his lot, even if it's less than he expected.

Execute Multiple Wills

This strategy calls for numerous redrafts of the will with only minor changes. With each new draft, you revoke the former wills. If the latest will is successfully challenged, the courts will rely on the revoked will that preceded it. With the multiple execution strategy, the will that preceded it should say basically the same thing, as should several versions of the will before that. With so many layers of the same will to contest, the challenger may drop the fight. This type of strategy is most effective for people who have dramatically changed their will in a way that will undoubtedly make someone unhappy—say, reducing the children's share in order to give more to the new spouse. It can be very tricky to execute, however, and should be done only with great care—preferably with the guidance of an attorney who has done it before. Again, the goal is to execute multiple wills with changes so minor that each new will says essentially the same thing as the one before it.

Also, if you are going to implement this strategy, you need to be sure that you properly revoke each of your former wills. If you fail to do this, you will have more than one valid will, which can cause serious problems for those who would need to establish your "true" will and true intentions.

Create a Living Trust

Revocable living trusts are another way to lessen the risk of a will contest. With a living trust, the trustee retains ownership of the assets when you die. So the assets in the trust avoid probate (although not estate taxes). The trustee can dole out the assets to your intended heirs without public scrutiny. In other words, the trustee can abide by your wishes in private, without having to notify your other heirs. Anyone not named in the trust who wants a piece of the action would first have to locate the trust—which can take time and money since, unlike the will, these things aren't publicly available—and then bring a lawsuit against the trust. Trusts aren't invincible to will contests, but they can provide an extra layer of protection. (See chapter 8 for more information on living trusts.)

Prove Competency

A common tactic for contesting a will is to claim that the deceased lacked the ability to draft a legally binding will, what is known in legal terms as testamentary capacity. It can be very hard to win a case based on testamentary capacity since all that's really needed in order to be of sound mind to draft a will is an understanding of the assets, the heirs involved, and the plan for disposition of the property.

Still, it's best that the lawyer hired to draft the will test for competency if any doubt might be cast on the mental capacity of the testator. How an attorney will test for capacity will vary. Some may request that the testator see a doctor and have the doctor assess capacity; others will ask a series of questions and record the answers.

Avoid the Perception of Undue Influence

A will can also be set aside if it is deemed to be the result of undue influence, or pressure and coercion. Say, for example, a daughter is taking care of her father. One day she reads his will and learns that he is leaving the house, where they both live, equally to all the children. She threatens to leave him to care for himself unless he changes his will so that she alone gains control of the house. She even goes with him to the lawyer's office to redraft the will. This daughter probably wouldn't believe her actions constitute undue influence. She would think she was demanding that her father do the right thing. The state, however, may see it differently if the other children bring her actions to the court's attention.

It's always best, when drafting a will, to avoid the appearance of undue influence. If you're planning, for example, to give the bulk of your assets to your daughter, at the expense of your other children, you should avoid hiring your daughter's lawyer to consult with you on your estate plan, having her present when you draft or sign the will, or—some attorneys would say—even allowing her to drive you to the attorney's office.

Properly Draft the Will

An improperly executed will can be thrown out of court in a second. To prevent your wishes from being thrown out on a technicality, make sure everything is done according to the letter of the law.

DICTIONARY

Testamentary capacity: The mental competency to execute a will at the time it is signed and witnessed. To have testamentary capacity, the person signing the will must understand the nature of making a will, have a general idea of what assets and property he or she possesses, and know who are the members of his or her immediate family, or the natural heirs.

Undue influence: Pressure used by an heir or potential heir to force the testator to execute a will leaving assets to that heir's benefit. The key to undue influence is proving that the influence was so great, the testator lost the ability to exercise individual judgment and felt he or she had no choice but to give in to the pressure.

CHAPTER 7

YOUR PERSONAL EFFECTS NEED A HOME, TOO

WHY THEFT IS OFTEN THE UNFORTUNATE SOLUTION

When will and estate disputes make the news, they almost always revolve around fights over significant sums of money or stakes in a family business. In reality, however, estate disputes often occur over things of little or no monetary value, like Mom's book of secret recipes or Dad's war memorabilia. The reason we don't hear about these fights is that they rarely make it to the inside of a courtroom. Indeed, the items of dispute are often not worth what it costs to hire a lawyer to duke it out—at least not in terms of dollars and cents.

Yet it's important to note that disputes over personal effects can cause rifts just as serious as those involving millions of dollars.

If you really want to maintain the family peace when you die, you will take as much care dividing your personal things as you do your money.

One reason problems often arise over personal effects is that people tend to divide their possessions in the same way they divide their monetary assets: equally. It's common for a simple will to say something like, "I want the house and half my property to go to my husband, Jake. I want the other half of my property to be divided equally among my three children, Michael, Mark, and Michelle." There's often no way to be equal about the distribution of personal effects in practice, however. You may have five things of equal value to give to your five children, but only one that has been passed on through generations. Dad may have only two war medals, and Mom probably has just one wedding ring. How do you decide which child gets to be the keeper of the family heirlooms?

FINDERS KEEPERS, LOSERS WEEPERS

When personal effects are not carefully divided, heirs often turn to theft as the solution. Consider: All your kids know that you have just one wedding ring. They also know that you didn't make any provisions about who should get it when you die. Your daughter Sally thinks she should get the ring because she's the oldest. She also knows, however, that her younger sister Anne wants the ring, too. Sally, feeling strongly that she deserves the ring as the oldest child, goes to your house before anyone else gets there and takes it. While she's there, she grabs a few other things she's always wanted, including the silverware and a hand-carved jewelry box.

It's hard to swallow, but it happens all the time, estate lawyers say. It's not limited to kids of shady or criminal character, either. Folks who pilfer their dead relatives' possessions are often perfectly upstanding citizens who would never otherwise consider stealing anything. When it comes to a beloved relative's things, however, people often truly believe that they have a right to certain items. Someone like Sally probably thinks that if only Mom had considered it before she died, she would certainly have given the item to Sally and not Anne, who isn't very careful with her own jewelry. These beliefs may even be true. Perhaps Mom would have given the ring to Sally, worried that Anne would lose it. Regardless of how true Sally's perceptions may be, the theft will create a lot of bad feelings between the two siblings.

Some people feel such a strong conviction that they deserve certain possessions that they won't even deny the theft. Indeed, they probably don't consider it theft. When Mrs. Wilson died, her two daughters went to her house looking for a bracelet she used to wear. It was one of the only things of value Mrs. Wilson had when she died. When the sisters discovered that the bracelet was gone, they questioned their brother about it. He readily admitted that he had already claimed the bracelet for himself. Needless to say, the siblings argued, but the brother held fast in his claim, stating that the bracelet was rightfully his. One of the sisters eventually sought legal advice on how to get the bracelet back, but her lawyer suggested she not pursue any legal action since it would cost more than the value of the bracelet. The Wilson sisters finally gave in. They had little choice. Their relationship with their brother, however, remained severely damaged.

Of course, theft is always a possibility when you leave your prized possessions in an unsafe place, such as a dresser drawer in your bedroom. When you pass away, your home may be filled with people coming in and out to share their condolences with your family. You have to be very careful about giving greedy relatives easy access to your valuables. Theft is also more likely when a family fails to talk about it beforehand. Had Mrs. Wilson told all her children before she died that she wanted the bracelet to go to her older daughter, her son still may have taken it—although it's less likely he would have admitted so readily to having done it. On the other hand, had Mrs. Wilson clearly told her daughters that she wanted her son to have the bracelet, they may have been angry, but they would not have been able to accuse him of theft.

IT'S EASY: JUST ASK WHO WANTS WHAT

One of the best ways to avoid fights and confusion over personal possessions is to simply ask who wants what while you're still alive. This strategy works best for older people, preferably those with grown children. (If your kids are still young, asking what they want to remember you by when you die will probably just frighten them.) A lot of retired people, on the other hand, are in the perfect position to not only start asking who wants what, but also start giving those things away. Why? Well, retirement often leads to downsizing. It's a time when couples move to smaller residences, throw out a lot of their old possessions, and start buying new things. Very likely, you're already asking your family members if they want some of your old things, so why limit it to things you would otherwise just throw away? If you have things of value that you want to pass down eventually, you might as well start doing it now.

With people living so long these days, it often doesn't make sense to hold on to your prized possessions until you die. By the time you pass, your kids could be well into retirement themselves. They will probably be considering who is going to be the beneficiary of their own possessions. You may, for example, not wear a lot of your jewelry anymore. Why not just give it to your daughters now? Also, why should you bother lugging that old mahogany desk—the one that was custom-built for your great-grandfather—to your new home when it doesn't match the furniture anyway? Why not give it to your son, who has been eyeing it ever since he bought his own home?

> **LOOK OUT!** If you give away your belongings in life, you want to be aware of triggering the gift tax—a federal tax imposed on large wealth transfers. This can include money and personal property such as art, furniture, and jewelry. Not all transfers are taxable. As a general rule, you want to research the gift tax if you plan to give any individual person gifts worth more than $12,000 in any given year. (See chapter 14 for more information.)

If you don't want to give it away yet, you should still consider asking who wants what. Start by allowing your closest heirs (such as your children) to choose first. Once they have selected the things they want, you can offer the remaining items to the next circle of heirs, like your siblings. After that, extend the offer to the next circle—say, your nieces and nephews. If more than one heir of the same circle wants the same item, you can resolve the situation by flipping a coin or picking a name out of a hat.

If your relatives choose things that you prefer to keep in your possession for the time being, you can still earmark their choices by labeling each item. When you pass, it will be clear to the executor and to all the other relatives to whom your things should go. You can also write out a list of who gets what on a piece of paper. Just be careful about attaching this sort of paper to your will. If you pass along specific items of personal property through the will, you could be creating a lot of additional work for the executor, who may have to get the items appraised.

Generally speaking, you want to include the valuable things, like jewelry, in your will. Everything else can be passed along through informal means. The downside to this, of course, is that your wishes may not be legally enforced. Generally speaking, however, the family abides by the deceased's wishes so long as they're in writing.

One of the reasons people don't ask is because they're afraid that if more than one person wants the same item, it will cause a fight. Again, you can diplomatically resolve disputes by flipping a coin or picking a name out of a hat. Certainly, it's better that they resolve this dilemma now while you're still around to act as the judge or mediator than to allow them to fight over it indefinitely when you're gone.

What Nobody Wants Can Land in the Trash

When you walk into Englishtown Used Furniture, an antiques shop in Englishtown, New Jersey, one of the first things you notice are the hauntingly beautiful antique wedding photographs that fill the store. You can also find correspondence—in the form of tattered letters—between husbands and wives, among other tantalizing personal items that may make you feel like a bit of a Peeping Tom.

So who are these people who have lost their most personal belongings to Sunday antiques shoppers? Perry Rosenblum, owner of the store, doesn't always know. He obtains these items through heirs and others, who have been put in charge of the items after someone has died. Executors, heirs, and others call him when they want homes cleared. He pays a fee to haul away what's available. He generally aims for the big stuff, like furniture, but often walks away with everything under the sun, including military correspondence, birth certificates, immigration papers, and travel memorabilia.

Mr. Rosenblum says the things people leave behind no longer shock him (although his wife still gets emotional sometimes when she sees how people's things have been neglected). Over the years, he and his wife have collected millions of photographs and other belongings that their owners probably held very dear to their hearts. So many things are left behind, in fact, that the Rosenblums can't hold on to everything they acquire and have to throw the bulk of them away. "There's just too many of them," Mr. Rosenblum said.

It can happen to your estate, too. Don't assume that your heirs will take care of your personal possessions when you die. They may not want your things, or they may not know where to find them. Whether heirs are able to collect personal belongings can also depend on how diligent the executor is in making sure people know what's available, especially for heirs who live far away.

Once—or at least one time that Mr. Rosenblum knows of—an executor deliberately asked that the deceased's belongings be hauled away before the heirs had an opportunity to collect. Why? In this case, it was a bit of revenge. The executor was a former neighbor of the deceased who, while growing up, had always thought of the deceased as a poor woman who needed the help of all her neighbors, including his own mother. Indeed, his mother was among many in the neighborhood who had taken care of her, giving her clothes and food, especially at the holidays. When the woman died, the former neighbor was named executor in place of his mother, who also had died. He soon discovered that the poor, helpless neighbor was actually wealthier than the people who had been supporting her, including his own mother, and that she'd been sending money to her relatives abroad for years. He properly distributed the assets to her family, as stated in the will. He loathed the thought, however, of spending any more time protecting her assets than he absolutely had to after discovering what he felt had been a lifelong deceit.

Of course, that's an extreme case. Most people name their spouse or another close relative to be the executor, and can feel confident that nothing will be sold or tossed in the trash before everyone of importance gets a chance to sift through it. However, if something is really important to you, and you don't want it to land up in the trash or an antiques store, try finding someone to take it while you're alive.

Still, in addition to all the reasons listed above, you might also find that none of your intended beneficiaries want your stuff. Sure, they may want what they think is valuable, but that won't necessarily be the same things you find worth preserving. Once you know nobody wants something you find of value, you can at least make separate arrangements so that your treasured belongings don't wind up trashed or sold. Perhaps you can give your unwanted things to charity or to a museum.

Collectibles are a good example of the kind of things that people should make arrangements for before they die, says Elaine Bloom, a personal organizer from Maplewood, New Jersey, who also cleans out estates. As a collector of science fiction books, Ms. Bloom knows how common it is for relatives to shrug off an obscure collection. If you learn ahead of time, however, that nobody in the family wants your stamp collection or your Depression-era magazines, you can at least find someone who does—perhaps a fellow collector or even a group that can use or preserve the items. Of course, you can always let your heirs sell the collection and divide the proceeds, but you may as well do that on your own and benefit directly.

PART II

ADVANCED PLANNING

Now that you've familiarized yourself with the basics of estate planning, it's time to consider some advanced techniques. In this section, I'll discuss the ins and outs of probate—the court proceedings that follow when you die with a will. I'll also talk about how you might avoid probate, if you so choose. Later, you will learn how you can control your heirs' inheritance. We'll also explore how you can plan for someone to take control of your health care or your finances if you ever become unable to do those things for yourself.

In a nutshell, we'll explore more technical topics of estate planning, including living trusts, ongoing trusts, probate, estate taxes, powers of attorney, health care proxies, and much more. Most likely, those terms mean nothing to you, but they will soon.

These topics may sound a little obscure and mechanical. In fact, they are very much related to some basic human concerns, such as the following:

- Will your children get any of your money if your spouse remarries?
- How do you know if you want to avoid probate?
- Are there ways to make probate easier?
- Who will take care of your beloved pets if you die before they do?
- How do you prevent your child from becoming a good-for-nothing trust-fund baby?

- Who will take care of your assets if you become incapacitated?

Still, estate planning is a legal field, and so there are many arcane legal terms and phrases that you will need to familiarize yourself with in order to get through the next few chapters. Generally speaking, these aren't tough concepts. Plus, once you have a good grasp of what you can do, you can construct your own plan—one that suits your own personal wants and needs.

CHAPTER 8

A WILL, A LIVING TRUST, OR BOTH?

BREAKING DOWN THE MYTHS OF TRUSTS

Before you open your laptop and start drafting your will, you should consider the main will alternative: the revocable living trust, also known as a revocable inter vivos trust.

The living trust is a wealth transfer tool, just like a will. The main goal is the same—to get your assets and property into the hands of your heirs when you die—but the process is somewhat different. In order to decide whether you want a will, a living trust, or both, you need to know how a living trust is different from a will and whether these differences better suit your needs or not.

DICTIONARY

Living, or inter vivos, trust: A trust that becomes active while you are still alive.

Testamentary trust: A type of trust that is created through a will. As such, it becomes active only after the trust creator dies.

Revocable trust: The terms of a revocable trust can be revoked or changed whenever the trust creator wants and for any reason.

Irrevocable trust: The terms of an irrevocable trust cannot be changed once the trust is activated.

WHY HAVE A LIVING TRUST?

• *Probate is costly in both time and money:* The cost of probate depends on where you live and the number of assets you have to be probated. In some states, costs can be high, especially for people with lots of money. If you're worried that probate will be a long and expensive process, you can reduce some of the hassle by placing your assets in a living trust.

• *You want to keep the value of your assets private:* Since the property owned by a living trust passes directly to your heirs without the interference of probate court, the process can remain private. With probate, an inventory of your assets will be made public record, as will the names of your heirs. If you want to keep this information confidential, you should consider a living trust.

• *You fear a will contest:* Living trusts aren't immune from challenge, but they do add a few extra layers of protection that cannot be offered by a will. Probate courts, by their very nature, are open to hearing complaints about how you distributed your assets. By transferring your property through a private living trust, you keep the process private, thus reducing the possibility that anyone will come after your assets. Also, anyone who chooses to contest the trust will have to go to the trouble of filing a lawsuit.

• *You own property in more than one state:* If you own property in more than one state, chances are that your will could be subject to probate in each state, increasing the hassle and the cost. By placing those assets in a living trust, you can avoid this problem.

• *You want to give someone control of your assets if you become incapacitated:* Most of the benefits associated with a living trust thus far have to do with avoiding probate. A living trust can also be a good way to hand over control of your assets should you become unable to handle them yourself. Without a living trust—or a power of attorney (see chapter 12)—the courts would have to appoint someone to manage your property, which can be time-consuming and expensive.

WHY YOU MIGHT NOT WANT A LIVING TRUST

• *Probate may be cheap and easy:* Living trusts are often touted as money-saving vehicles. This isn't always true. Indeed, the cost of setting up a living trust can be higher than that to write a will and settle the estate, especially for people with small estates. If you feel confident that probate in your state will be a relatively simple and cheap process, you should stick with a straight will. Also, if you have a lot of money, but the bulk of your assets is tied up in accounts that already escape probate such as a 401(k), probate might be the better option.

• *You never want to look at your estate plan again:* One downfall with living trusts is that they can require a lot of maintenance. If you're the kind of person who wants to put it away and never look at it again, then a trust is not for you. Once you establish the trust, you have to go through the motions of formally transferring property to the trust, which requires writing letters to banks, brokerage firms, and human resource departments. Every time you purchase a new property you should buy it in the name of the trust. Also, every time you inherit property, you should have it transferred to the trust.

• *You could lose your homestead exemption:* Some states have laws that allow homeowners to reduce their property taxes through what is known as a homestead exemption. If you place your home in a living trust, however, you could lose this exemption, depending on the rules of your state.

• *You have lots of creditors:* When your assets pass through probate, creditors are notified and invited to file claims. They generally have a few months from the date the court appoints the executor to file their claims. If creditors fail to file claims within the established period, they can lose their right to collect on their debts. Living trusts generally have no such powers to force creditors to file claims promptly or say good-bye forever.

How Does This Trust-Thing Work, Anyhow?

The concept of a will is pretty easy to grasp. You write your wishes on a piece of paper and the court ensures that they are met after you die, using the help of a court-appointed executor.

But what about the living trust? How does it work, and how do you ensure that it's properly executed?

A proper trust always has the same setup. First, it has three parties involved. The person who sets up the trust is the donor, also known as the trustor or the settler. The person the donor hires to be in charge of managing the trust property and doling out the distributions is the trustee. Finally, there's the beneficiary, or the person named by the donor to benefit from the money in the trust. Of course, there may be more than one person in each of these roles. Some of these parties can also be interchangeable. The donor, for example, might name him- or herself to also be the trustee, which is the common setup for a revocable living trust. However, it's a rule of thumb that a sole trustee cannot also be the sole beneficiary. Also, no one person can be all three.

A traditional trust scenario works like this: You, the donor, retain equitable title to the property, but give legal title to the trustee. To put it simply, this means that you own the property, but the trustee is legally responsible for managing it according to your wishes. Also, while the trustee has legal responsibility for the money, he or she can't benefit from it. The trustee cannot, for example, withdraw the money for a vacation in Bermuda unless the donor wishes it. Put another way, the donor hands over the property, the trustee has control of the property but can't use it for him- or herself, and the beneficiary can use the property but only according to the terms outlined by the donor.

The above concept helps explain why money in a trust can avoid probate. The trustee has legal rights to the property; technically speaking, it's not part of the donor's estate. Since the donor retains equitable title, however, he or she would still have to pay taxes on the money, including estate taxes after death.

You may be wondering: *How is the trust enforced?* Well, the courts enforce trusts, just as with a will. Only the court won't get involved unless someone, such as the beneficiary, brings a problem to the court's attention. (With a will, the court is pretty much involved whether you like it or not.) The beneficiary might claim, for example, that the trustee neglected his or her duties. Under the rules that govern trusts, trustees have very specific responsibilities and are expected to abide by these duties as they manage their trusts.

MYTHS ABOUT LIVING TRUSTS

- *You do not need a will:* Even if you have a revocable trust, you should still draft a will. The main purpose of the will for people with living trusts should be to tie up any loose ends. A will that's tied to a living trust is generally called a pour-over will, because it asks that all the property not already in the living trust be poured into it. People with minor children also need a will if they want to name someone to be guardian in case they die.

- *You will always avoid probate:* A living trust helps you avoid probate on the assets within the trust. If everything you own is in the trust, you will avoid probate. If you've left probate property outside the living trust, however, it will still have to go to probate, unless you can use an affidavit to transfer the assets to the rightful heirs. One of the biggest dangers of living trusts is that people fail to update their trusts when they acquire new assets. As a result, they have to pay the costs of probate in addition to the costs they paid to draft the probate-avoidance trust.

- *You can avoid estate taxes:* One of the biggest myths about living trusts is that, because they help you avoid probate, you can also escape death taxes that might be due to federal or state governments. This simply isn't true. Certain trust structures—working together with a living trust—can help you reduce taxes through clever maneuvering of your assets, but a simple revocable living trust isn't one of them. Indeed, a simple revocable living trust will do absolutely nothing to lower your estate tax bill.

• *Creditors can't touch your living trust assets:* If the trust were irrevocable, you might be able to protect the trust property from creditors, but you would also lose control of the property within the trust. A simple revocable living trust does nothing to protect your assets from creditors, especially when you, the donor, also serve as trustee. Indeed, if there isn't enough money in the probate estate to pay creditors, the creditors will come after the assets in the living trust.

• *Trusts are cheaper:* Again, while it's true that a trust can save on probate costs, it's not necessarily true that a living trust will be cheaper than going through probate. In some cases, it may be more expensive. You have to do your research to determine what the costs of drafting a trust agreement will be in comparison with probate in your state for an estate of your size. Remember, if you get a trust, you will want to factor in the cost of drafting a will in addition to the trust agreement. If you have assets that need to go through probate, you will have to cough up court fees and other probate costs. Generally speaking, trusts cost more up front and wills cost more down the road, when the assets pass through probate. Which route is ultimately cheaper, however, will depend on your individual circumstances.

• *Heirs get their inheritance faster:* The trustee of a living trust has many of the same responsibilities as an executor of a will, which can delay the inheritance. The trustee can distribute the assets of the trust immediately—unlike with the will—but this assumes there are no additional taxes or debts, and that the distributions were made correctly. A good trustee will want to take the time to first identify the assets, render an accounting of the estate, pay creditors (or at least wait for the executor to pay them), and file and pay death and income taxes. Certainly, if you plan well, your beneficiaries can have access to living trust assets much sooner than

with probate proceedings. If problems crop up, however—
say, a disappointed family member files a lawsuit against the
trust—they will further delay the inheritance distribution. As
such, it can take the same amount of time as administering
a probate estate.

LOOK OUT! Living Trusts Are a Big Business

Be wary of high-pressure sales tactics for living trusts.
In order to sell you a living trust, salespeople may mis-
represent or lie about the benefits of this tool, claiming
that it can help you avoid all probate and administrative
costs or keep your assets out of the hands of creditors. In
some cases, they may sell living trusts that aren't even
prepared by a lawyer, and yet charge more than what a
professional attorney would charge.

The Federal Trade Commission went after Michael P.
McIntyre, an officer and director of The Administrative
Company and Pre-Paid Legal Services,* for distributing
false statements about living trusts. The sales literature,
according to allegations by the FTC, exaggerated the
benefits of living trusts, as in the following statement:
"With a living trust, your family will not have to go
through probate, and can avoid paying expensive probate fees and costs." The FTC also took issue with state-

*In the Matter of The Administrative Company, a Texas Corporation,
Michael P. McIntyre, individually and as an officer and director of The
Administrative Company, and Pre-Paid Legal Services, Inc., an Okla-
homa Corporation, Docket No. C-3729.

ments such as the following: "A living trust prevents a will contest," and, "Is There Anything Bad About a Living Trust? No. There is nothing bad about a Living Trust." The FTC settled with Pre-Paid Legal Services in a manner that did "not constitute an admission . . ." of violations of law. Still, the parties named agreed to stop making certain statements about living trusts, such as that they are appropriate for every consumer and that they cannot be challenged, according to a 1997 consent order to cease and desist issued by the FTC.

If that's not bad enough, consider the story of Alliance for Mature Americans. The average age of an Alliance client was seventy-three, according to the complaint, which was filed by the state attorney general's office and the State Bar of California.* The salespeople received about two days of training, but identified themselves as "certified trust advisers." Meanwhile, some of the trust documents they sold didn't comply with statutory requirements, and the company failed to follow through with various requirements to complete the trust process, according to the complaint. The alleged scam didn't stop there. The sales force used people's living trust documents to gain information about clients' assets and then pressure them into buying expensive annuities. Alliance sold more than ten thou-

---

The People of the State of California and the State Bar of California v. Fremont Life Insurance Company, Case No. BC 153983.

sand living trust packages and more than $200 million in annuities, according to the complaint. The attorney general and the state bar association settled with Alliance for Mature Americans in a manner that allowed the Alliance to "not admit to any wrongdoing," according to a 1997 press release by the State Bar of California. Still, the parties agreed to pay $1 million in restitution to individuals who purchased living trusts from Alliance for Mature Americans after August 1, 1991, and to stop selling and preparing living trusts.

Of course, it's not just living trusts that salespeople find attractive. All kinds of trusts are touted as having magical powers to avoid this or that. One of the oldest scams is a trust that promises protection for everything under the sun, from creditors to taxes. These trusts, known as pure or constitutional trusts, are based on the assertion that the U.S. Constitution doesn't allow the state to impair the "obligation of contracts." As such, a trust is beyond the reach of the law. If you get such a trust, and the IRS catches on, you or your heirs will be required to pay back taxes for as long as the trust was in existence.

I'M STILL CONFUSED. DO I NEED A WILL, A TRUST, OR BOTH?

After reading about living trusts, you might still be asking yourself, *Which instrument is right for me?* Again, most people should have a will, if only as a backup piece of paper that catches any assets left unnamed in the living trust. Also, the will is generally the only legal means for nominating a person to act as a guardian for your minor children, so if you have young children you may indeed need a will. If you're young and don't have many assets, you are probably better off with a simple will. If you have a larger estate, however, consider the benefits of a living trust. Of course, you still need to ask yourself if the benefits of a living trust are right for you:

- Do you want to pass on certain assets without the hassle of court supervision?
- Do you want the protection a living trust can provide if you become incapacitated?
- Will you be diligent enough to update the trust as you acquire new assets?
- Do you want to provide an extra layer of protection against jilted heirs?

CHAPTER 9

THE TRUTH ABOUT PROBATE

IS IT REALLY SO BAD?

In order to fully understand whether you need a will, a living trust, or both, you have to understand probate. The main thing people want to know when choosing between a will and a living trust is: *Is probate really so bad?* Unfortunately—as with most things—the answer isn't cut-and-dried. In some cases, it can be quite easy. Indeed, there are a number of ways that you might obtain permission for simplified probate proceedings. If you can benefit from these proceedings, probate will certainly be faster, cheaper, and overall less hassle than the traditional sort.

First, let's explore the workings of traditional probate.

WHAT IS THIS THING CALLED PROBATE?

Probate is a court-supervised process intended to ensure that a deceased person's property and assets are properly distributed according to the law. If you draft a legally binding will, the probate court will ensure that your wishes are enforced within the law. If there's no will, the court will require that the property be distributed according to state law.

In order to do this, the court will require that someone step up to the plate to act as your executor or personal representative. Again, if you named someone in your will to take on this position, your wishes will be granted. Otherwise, the court will have to appoint someone. The executor is responsible for dealing with the court and your beneficiaries, and for protecting and distributing your assets. Generally, the court will require that the executor keep in touch through constant documentation of the process, including an inventory of the assets and property of the estate, lists of beneficiaries, and receipts showing that distributions to heirs were received.

The court is also there to make sure that your will follows the laws of the state. This means ensuring that minor children have a caretaker, that outstanding debts are paid, that taxes are paid, and that rightful heirs receive their inheritance. If the will was drafted so that you disinherit your spouse, for example, the probate court will set things straight.

One good aspect of probate is that it has a set of procedures to see to it that everything is taken care of before the court will sign off on your estate as being settled. If relatives start arguing over the distribution of assets, the court will step in to resolve disputes. This close supervision has its downside. In trying to ensure that all your rightful heirs have received their due, the court opens the path for jilted heirs to contest your distributions. In ensuring that your will is legal, it might throw out an otherwise legitimate will that was drafted incorrectly—thus throwing off your entire plan.

Here's a list of some of the common tasks your executor could face in probate:

- *Ask to be named executor:* The executor named in your will (or whoever wants the job if you failed to draft a will) wants to get the court's permission to act as the executor. Generally this means filing an application, or petition, with the court. To do this, the executor needs to compile information about the beneficiaries named in the will, along with a death certificate and information about your assets. The original will also needs to be filed with the court. After an application is filed, a hearing date will be set for the court to say yea or nay to the executor. (Again, your choice of executor should be approved unless he or she is unwilling or unable to do the job.)

• *Prove the validity of the will:* When the executor files your will with the court, evidence that the will is valid may also need to be provided. If you created a self-proving affidavit when you signed your will, this should be enough to prove its validity. Otherwise, your executor may have to get a statement from one or more of your witnesses. Witnesses may also be required to visit the court. Every state has its own rules. The benefit to this procedure is that the court is there to intervene if there's evidence that the will is a fake concocted by a greedy heir, or an outdated document that doesn't reflect your most recent intentions. On the flip side, probate courts are also known for turning down wills that do adequately reflect the deceased's wishes, but simply haven't been drafted properly according to the letter of the law. Again, you need to follow certain rules when drafting your will in order to make sure it's legal. A small mistake, such as the wrong number of witnesses, could totally invalidate your will in the eyes of the court.

• *Inform interested parties of the hearing:* Before the court officially appoints your executor, it wants to know that there are no major objections. Thus, your executor will need to notify all beneficiaries named in your will, as well as all your natural beneficiaries (people who should inherit under law) and your debtors. In addition to personal calls and letters, a death notice should be published in the local paper.

• *Identify, secure, and value all property:* The executor will also want to locate all your property to make sure it's safe and secure. If property needs to be managed—real estate, for instance—the executor should take the appropriate steps. He or she will also want to create an inventory of the property, including values. In some cases, professional appraisals must be ordered.

• *Collect any money owed to the estate:* Part of identifying and securing the estate involves collecting money owed, such as outstanding income checks and life insurance.

• *Pay all expenses, debts, and taxes:* The executor will also want to pay any debts and taxes owed by the deceased, including outstanding utility bills and credit card debts. In addition to paying your debts, he or she should end all regular billings, including newspaper and magazine subscriptions, cable television, and any unnecessary insurance premiums.

• *Distribute the property to the heirs:* Your executor will also need to supervise final distribution of assets to the heirs. Generally, this is done after all debts are paid and enough time has elapsed that no additional creditors or unhappy heirs can come after the assets in the estate. Also, the executor should collect receipts upon delivery of each item to prove that the assets, property, or personal items were delivered.

• *Close the estate:* To close the estate, the executor will have to submit a report of his or her activities to the court. This report, often referred to as an accounting, should demonstrate that all debts have been paid, the assets were distributed to the beneficiaries, and everything was accounted for. This process ends probate and releases your executor from his or her duties.

As you can see, probate is a process intended to make sure that no stone is left unturned before finally closing the estate. This kind of close scrutiny has its pros and cons, all of which you will need to weigh before deciding whether you want a probate-avoidance trust.

The Time

How long probate takes will (you guessed it) vary by state. It will also depend greatly on the complexity of the estate, the efficiency of the executor, and the thoroughness of the plan provided by the decedent. An executor who has to sift through drawers of papers to find the right documents and the key to the safe-deposit box will probably require more time to close the estate than the executor who finds all the documents in order in one place. Likewise, the executor who has to deal with will contests will probably be less swift in settling the estate than the executor who meets with satisfied beneficiaries. Generally speaking, a straightforward probate proceeding can last between six months and one year.

Don't get the wrong idea—probate doesn't necessarily require limitless appearances before a judge. In some cases, your executor might never have to see the inside of the courtroom. Indeed, if your executor is lucky, his or her main contact with the court will be through lots of paperwork, not appearances before a judge.

The Cost

The cost of probate will vary by state, too. In some states, the county will set its own fees. In others, probate fees will fluctuate based on the value of the assets. People with lots of assets, therefore, may find it cheaper to use a probate-avoidance trust. The cost of probate will also depend on how much help the executor needs and how long the process takes. The executor may need to hire a lawyer to assist with the process and an appraiser to value the estate property. He or she may also need to hire an accountant and someone to help file the taxes.

Probate is often portrayed as a costly and bureaucratic process that causes heirs unnecessary pain and heartache. In some states, this may be true—but not in all. If you are truly concerned about probate, you want to consider placing your assets in a living trust, which is another legal way to transfer your wealth after death. (See chapter 8 for more information.)

Posting a Bond

Your executor may be asked by the court to post a bond in order to serve. This money is intended to act as insurance against any losses caused by the executor. If you don't want your executor to have to post this bond, you can request in your will that no bond be posted. This practice is very common, since most people don't want their executors—who are generally doing the deceased a favor—to go through the hassle of posting a bond.

Look! A Simplified Version

Before you make a decision between a will and a living trust, know that there are simplified probate proceedings that can reduce the time, cost, and hassle of probate. Of course, some of these proceedings may be available to you only if you have a small estate or have most of your property tied up in non-probate assets, such as joint tenancy real estate property or even living trusts.

Generally speaking, there are two main forms of simplified probate: independent administration and summary probate. There is also the possibility for beneficiaries in certain states to avoid probate through the use of affidavits.

Independent Administration

Some states are allowing what's known as independent administration to simplify probate proceedings for uncomplicated estates. This type of administration gives executors the freedom to undertake many tasks, such as paying debts and selling property, without the burden of prior court approval. In other words, your executor can settle the estate through paperwork, free of court hearings. As the name implies, it's more independent. It's also known to be less costly than formal probate. A formal administration would be required, for example, when an heir contests the will. In such a case, the courts would want to monitor every move to make sure the conflict is properly resolved.

Summary Probate

Summary probate—also known as simplified probate—is basically another simplified version of formal probate. Again, it's more independent and also less costly than formal probate; it's allowed for small estates that are expected to be hassle-free.

The main difference between summary probate and independent administration is that summary probate generally requires that the estate be of a small size, which is defined differently by each state. With independent administration, the size of the estate may not matter as much as the assurance that it can be settled without disputes.

Affidavits

A number of states, including Arizona, California, Iowa, Maine, Nevada, South Carolina, Texas, Utah, Virginia, and Washington, allow heirs to use affidavits to gain access to assets in place of probate proceedings. Use of affidavits is simple and essentially seeks to transfer title of property from the decedent to the beneficiary directly through the financial institution that holds the assets. Beneficiaries just prepare an affidavit statement and present it to the bank or other institution that owns the property. In some states, the affidavit must also be filed with the probate court.

Heirs can generally use affidavit proceedings to gain owner-ship of a decedent's bank accounts, brokerage accounts, or other property. Few states allow heirs to file an affidavit for real estate, however. Some states require that the affidavit be signed before a notary public. Also, heirs would be wise to consult with the fi-nancial institution holding the assets before presenting an affi-davit. Some institutions will require different proof of ownership or a copy of the will or death certificate.

> **LOOK OUT!** An executor who has already started regu-lar probate proceedings generally will not qualify for a more streamlined process.

HOW CAN MY ESTATE QUALIFY FOR ONE OF THESE SIMPLIFIED PROCEDURES?

Whether or not you can benefit from any of these simplified procedures will depend on the rules of your state. Each state has adopted different forms of simplified probate, as well as its own set of qualifications for determining who might be eligible. Not every state offers all three of these procedures, and those that do may use different terminology. Some states use the term *unsu-pervised administration* to refer to independent administration. Florida, meanwhile, used to offer something called family admin-istration that operated much like summary probate, but benefited estates in which only direct descendants or ascendants were the beneficiaries.

In addition to the dollar amount an estate may need to qualify, there may be additional requirements. For example, some states permit certain kinds of simplified procedures only for people without a will or for estates without real estate.

Qualifying for simplified probate because you have a small estate doesn't necessarily mean that you're poor. It may just mean that you don't have a lot of probate property. Also, some states allow people to exclude sizable property, such as real estate, when configuring the size of the estate for probate. In fact, the small-estate rules offer people lots of opportunities to maintain large assets in non-probate form, such as joint ownership, and still qualify for small-estate probate for the few assets remaining.

Say, for example, that you live in Colorado. You would be allowed to pass on your estate by means of affidavits if the value of the probate estate is $50,000 or less. When calculating the value of the estate for affidavit proceedings in Colorado, you can exclude any non-probate property, including joint tenancy property and payable-on-death accounts. So, say you own a house jointly with your spouse, an IRA account, and a few bank certificates of deposit, all of which you have arranged to pass directly to your spouse as non-probate assets when you die. You also own a $45,000 brokerage account, which you plan to leave to your children—the only property you own that will pass through the will. Since your probate property falls beneath the $50,000 limit, your children would be able to file an affidavit with the brokerage firm and gain access to the account without having to go to court and file for probate. All of your heirs, therefore, will be able to avoid probate.

It's important that you know what simplified procedures are available in your state when drafting your will. While your executor will generally determine probate proceedings for your estate, there is some possibility that you can elect one of these procedures ahead of time.

Consider the story of the Hernandez family, who live in Texas.

Under Texas law, a testator can ask for independent administration in a will. If there is no will, independent administration can still be obtained, but only if all the heirs agree to it. Mr. Hernandez died without a will and all his heirs agreed to an independent administration—all except one: a daughter who was nowhere to be found. She had disappeared years before, and her family suspected that she had changed her name, and perhaps even her sex.

Finally, after months of searching for the missing heir, the family was able to prove that the daughter had been missing so long, it was reasonable to presume she was dead. The family was then granted the independent administration, but not after several months of fighting and paying attorney's fees. In the end, the family ended up spending roughly $12,000 in legal fees to settle their father's estate. Had Mr. Hernandez planned for his death and opted for an independent administration, the process could have been reduced to roughly $1,500.

TECH TALK: Having a lot of non-probate assets doesn't mean you should avoid writing a will. Certainly it's possible to plan effectively without ever drafting a will using living trusts, joint tenancy, and other probate-avoidance techniques—but it's not smart. A will is a good backup tool, something there to catch forgotten property. If your payable-on-death account beneficiaries die, for example, probate may be needed to decide who should get the money. Or if joint tenancy owners were to die simultaneously, ownership of the property would need to be directed by the will. Without a will, ownership would be decided by the state. Living trusts also work best in conjunction with a will. It can take time and effort to place assets in a trust. If you die before you get a chance to put all your property in the trust, the will would be able to direct who gets what upon your death. Having a will, even just as a backup piece of paper, can act as a safety net, catching anything that was accidentally left out or forgotten. As long as the assets being passed through the will are small enough, your heirs should still be able to avoid, or at least streamline, the probate process.

CHAPTER 10

THE ONGOING TRUST

CONTROLLING YOUR HEIRS FROM THE GRAVE

In addition to a will and a living trust, you might want to add an ongoing trust to your estate plan. This kind of trust allows you to control distributions and, in some cases, beneficiary behavior—a strategy known as controlling from the grave (not as spooky as it sounds). People who want ongoing trusts are usually faced with similar dilemmas. Here are some of the sentiments common among them:

- *I love my beneficiary, but I just don't trust him to do the right thing with the money.*
- *I love my beneficiary, but an outright gift is just out of the question. There are too many risks that the money will be mismanaged, misspent, or misdirected.*
- *I trust my beneficiary, but I want to decide how the money is spent.*
- *I love my beneficiary, but I don't want him to be corrupted by such a large inheritance.*

- *I trust my beneficiary, but I don't trust someone close to her.*

If any of these statements reflect your feelings, you want to consider an ongoing trust. Some reasons for wanting to maintain control are obvious. If you have a son with mental disabilities, you want to have someone manage his inheritance for him when you're gone. Or perhaps your daughter is a spendthrift, spending every dollar she gets on shoes, clothes, and parties with her friends.

Other reasons for wanting to maintain control are less obvious. Even if your grown daughter is financially responsible, you may worry that she could lose her inheritance to a spendthrift spouse. Or perhaps you are worried that your aging spouse is showing signs of deterioration and may not be able to manage the money you leave him or her down the road. Elder abuse is a common problem in this country, with greedy relatives, nurses, neighbors, and even perfect strangers latching on to vulnerable older people.

The ongoing trusts referred to here are different from the revocable living trust mentioned in chapter 8. A basic revocable living trust is a wealth transfer instrument. Much like a will, it dissolves after the wealth is properly transferred. Ongoing trusts, on the other hand, are designed so that they can last for years, or even generations, generally with the purpose of protecting heirs or protecting assets. Often, the two goals are intertwined. By controlling how a young heir manages his or her inheritance, you can protect your assets from being squandered or stolen while simultaneously sparing your heir the pain and suffering that come from a major loss.

TECH TALK: Most of the ongoing trusts discussed in this chapter are testamentary trusts. In other words, you would establish the trust as part of your will or living trust; it would become active only when you die. As such, you can change the terms of the trust as you please while you are alive. Once the trust becomes activated, however, it will become irrevocable. In other words, the terms of the trust can no longer be changed at that point.

Let's take a closer look at the benefits of ongoing trusts:

• *You can control distributions:* One of the main benefits of trusts is that you can control how you distribute your money after you die. A will generally lets you control who gets your money, but you can't, for example, control how it's distributed. You might wish to control distributions for a number of reasons, perhaps to protect your assets, or to protect your heirs. You might also want to impose your own beliefs, requiring heirs to spend your money the way you would have spent it had you been alive. Say, for example, that you have $1 million to leave to your only child, Cynthia, but you don't want to give it to her all at once lest she become too reliant on the money and never achieve success on her own. With a trust, you can distribute the $1 million in chunks, say, doling out $20,000 every five years, starting with the year you die. This way, Cynthia will still have to hustle to afford her current lifestyle, despite the inheritance. Or perhaps you want to ensure that your children go to college if you die before then. You can set up a trust with money allocated specifically for higher education purposes. If your beneficiaries go to college, they get the money to pay for tuition, books, and other expenses. If they don't attend college within a reasonable number of years, you can request that the money be distributed to another beneficiary, such as your alma mater.

• *You can protect your assets:* By putting your money in trust, you can also protect your assets, ensuring that wasteful or immature beneficiaries don't squander it, or that vulnerable beneficiaries don't lose it to greedy and unscrupulous people around them. Let's say you have $1 million to leave to your only son, Fritz. You're worried, however, that if you give him the money outright, he will spend it in a matter of months on a lifestyle of fun and leisure. By setting up a trust, you can restrict Fritz's spending to certain predetermined needs, such as rent, food, and education, thus preserving the money for purposes that you find acceptable. Trusts can also be beneficial for people who, while trustworthy and responsible in their own right, might lose the money to others. Elders are often taken advantage of by salespeople, or by greedy family members. If you're concerned, for example, that your money could end up in the hands of your husband's nurse, you might want to consider a trust. Even if you trust your heirs completely, you might not trust everyone around them. You may be worried, for example, that your son-in-law will seize your daughter's inheritance for one of his crackpot business ideas. A trust can keep him from tapping the money while still giving your daughter access to her inheritance.

• *You can avoid probate:* As discussed regarding revocable living trusts in chapter 8, you can also avoid probate with trusts. To do this, however, you would need to have a living trust, or one that has already been established during your life. A testamentary trust, or one that is created through a will, would require probate to become activated.

• *You can save taxes:* There's really no way to evade paying taxes (and be very wary of anyone making such a claim), but there are tricks you can use to reduce your tax liability using trusts. For example, trusts may let you reduce your tax liability by taking advantage of all available exemptions. (For information on using trusts to limit estate taxes, see chapter 14.)

How Trusts Work

In any discussion involving trusts, it's important to make one thing clear: They are just another estate planning tool, like a will, with their own rules and limitations. People often mistakenly believe that trusts, especially ongoing trusts, are magical entities that offer supreme protection from taxes, debtors, and the laws of the day. This simply isn't true. You cannot, for example, use trust money to commit crimes or to act against public policy. A trust established for the purpose of funding terrorists would be shut down if discovered, and the parties involved would be prosecuted.

If you're being sold a trust that seems to have magical powers of protection, be careful. It's probably a scam. Indeed, people who have been sold trusts on the premise that they could avoid taxes often find out the hard way—through back taxes and hefty IRS penalties—that they were duped.

A proper trust always has the same setup. First, it has three parties involved. The person who sets up the trust is the donor, also known as the trustor or the settler. The person the donor hires to be in charge of managing the trust property and doling out the distributions is the trustee. Finally, there's the beneficiary, or the person named by the donor to benefit from the money in the trust. Of course, there may be more than one person in each of these roles. Some of these parties can also be interchangeable.

The donor, for example, might name him- or herself to also be the trustee, which is the common setup for a revocable living trust.

A traditional trust scenario works like this: You, the donor, retain equitable title to the property, but give legal title to the trustee. To put it simply, this means that you own the property but the trustee is legally responsible for managing it according to your wishes. The trustee has legal responsibility for the money but can't benefit from it. The trustee cannot, for example, withdraw the money for a vacation unless the donor wishes it. Put another way, the donor hands over the property, the trustee has control of the property but can't use it for him- or herself, and the beneficiary can use the property but only according to the terms outlined by the donor.

The reason the money in a trust can avoid probate is that the trustee has legal rights to the property; technically speaking, it's not part of the donor's estate. Since the donor retains equitable title, however, he or she would still have to pay taxes on the money, including estate taxes after death.

To better picture how a trust works, try thinking of it like a bank vault. When setting up a trust, you're essentially opening a private bank vault and putting whatever you want in it for safekeeping. The trustee is the banker, or the person you hire to monitor the money in the vault and distribute it according to your wishes. The beneficiary, of course, is the person you named to benefit from the money placed in the private bank vault.

Now let's apply these rules to some common scenarios.

PROTECTING YOUR CHILD FROM BECOMING A LAZY BUM

Warren Buffett has reportedly said that he wants to give his kids enough money so that they feel they can do anything, "but not so much that they feel they could do nothing." Indeed, it can be tough to balance the two goals, especially if you have accumulated a lot of money and want to pass the bulk of it to your children.

If you are worried that leaving too much money to your children could encourage them to be lazy bums or trust-fund babies, you might want to control their distributions through a trust. For example, you could add language to the trust documents instructing the trustee to pay only for certain expenditures. You might choose to pay only for basic needs, such as food, shelter, and education. If your child wants a car or money for a vacation, he or she would have to earn the money. The idea is to encourage your children to make their own living while still providing them with an inheritance.

Another solution might be to dole out the money in short spurts, perhaps giving your child $50,000 or so every five years. Since nobody can live on just $10,000 a year, your child would need to get a job to supplement the trust income.

Trusts created to prevent beneficiaries from squandering their inheritances are often referred to as spendthrift trusts. They are created with very specific language that explains to the trustee what an appropriate distribution of the funds is.

Keep in mind that, despite the name, spendthrift trusts aren't just for ne'er-do-wells. They can also help responsible children who need protection from creditors, a divorce, or any problem that might result in a loss of their inheritance. They can be useful, for example, to people in professions in which lawsuits are common, such as doctors. Since the money in the trust does not legally belong to the trustee, creditors and others can have a hard time gaining access to it.

Instilling Your Values in Your Child

Some people want to set up trusts to instill their own values in their children. This type of trust is often referred to as an incentive trust. To create an incentive trust, you would add language to the trust documents instructing the trustee to make distributions to heirs according to certain accomplishments, such as educational or career goals. If you want to motivate your children to get an education, for example, you could tell the trustee to distribute a large lump sum to each child upon graduation. If you want to motivate your child to work, you might provide a financial match based on salary—$1 for every $2 your child earns, for example. In order not to penalize children who want respectable but low-paying jobs, you could also provide for additional compensation if they choose jobs that contribute to society, including teachers, social workers, and artists.

Incentive trusts can also keep family members in the family business by providing additional funds to anyone who keeps the business running. Entrepreneurs may want to ask that trustees make distributions to children who want to start a business.

Incentive trusts can also be used to discourage bad behaviors, such as drug use, alcoholism, or criminal activity. You may require the trustee to cut off any child engaged in criminal activity, or ask that the child be tested for drugs before distributions can be made.

LOOK OUT! Critics charge that incentive trusts can be damaging to children. How? Well, incentive, they argue, should come from within. External incentives, such as money, lead children to become motivated to earn more of the inheritance, not to achieve the goals you set out. Furthermore, if the goals you set out aren't in line with your children's desires, it could lead to depression. If you want your children to be motivated from within, you have to pass those lessons on when they're still young. If your grown children have failed to learn those lessons already, it may be too late.

When writing an incentive provision, be aware of certain pitfalls. For example, is it enough for your children to attend college to receive a distribution? You might also want to specify the kind of college they should attend—whether they need to attend a four-year university, say, or if a technical school can also qualify. What about grade point average? Should they be expected to meet a certain average or simply attend school, period? Also, should they be rewarded while attending school or only upon graduation—the point at which they have achieved the goal? If you provide a match for salary earned, you may want to consider adding a cap to the match so that a beneficiary who earns an unusually large salary doesn't deplete the trust. Also, you want to be careful not to punish children who cannot work because of a disability or because they need to take care of a disabled or terminally ill child or parent. Along the same lines, beware of punishing children who may need or want to give up work to raise a family full-time. Do you really want to disinherit a child for caring for his or her family?

PROTECTING THE INHERITANCE FROM BAD INVESTMENT DECISIONS

Here's another common dilemma: Your beneficiary may be completely trustworthy and responsible, but still not know how to properly manage an inheritance. This can be especially disconcerting if the amount being passed on is quite large.

Consider the story of a young man we'll call Marcus. Marcus

inherited several million dollars at the age of eighteen. It was an outright gift, so no controls had been placed on how he spent or invested his money. If he had wanted, Marcus could have chosen to blow it all before his nineteenth birthday. But he was a smart boy and chose to save it instead. With his parents guiding him, he kept the inheritance in bank accounts. He continued to work to earn his living and even dabbled in ideas for charitable contributions to better his community.

Still, Marcus was young and not so savvy in the ways of the world, especially when it came to investing. A former cousin by marriage had grown close to Marcus through the years. One day she suggested he invest in a business venture she was working on in her home country in South America. After some discussion, Marcus agreed to hand over a good chunk of his inheritance for this business venture. His family protested, but he trusted his cousin and believed he was helping her. On his cousin's suggestion, Marcus opened a joint bank account so that when she returned to her home country to visit the people involved in the project, she could tap the funds as needed.

Needless to say, all the money was gone from the account within a few weeks. Marcus never heard from his cousin again.

If you trust your beneficiary, but worry that he or she could fall prey to bad investment decisions as Marcus did, an ongoing trust with a more responsible third-party trustee can provide some protection. You can even name your beneficiary a co-trustee to ensure that he or she doesn't feel cut off from the inheritance.

A trust can also help your beneficiaries learn how to manage money. If your beneficiary is young, for example, you might create a trust that will hand out the inheritance in increments—say, every five years. This way, your beneficiary can slowly take control of the money. Any initial mistakes will be made with a limited amount of money and, hopefully, won't be repeated.

PROTECTING YOUR CHILD'S INHERITANCE FROM A SPOUSE

When your child gets married, his or her spouse becomes family. It makes sense that whatever your child inherits will be shared with your new son- or daughter-in-law. Still, there are some reasons you might consider placing restrictions on your child's inheritance with the goal of keeping the money out of the hands of the spouse.

Consider, for example, if your child is married to someone who's a bit of a bully when it comes to the family finances. You want your daughter's inheritance to be saved in case of an emergency, or to be reserved for special occasions such as a wedding or college education for your grandchild. Your daughter feels the same way. Still, you're worried about giving her the inheritance outright because your son-in-law, Raymond, is the boss of the house and controls all the finances. While your daughter says she will ensure the money is reserved for the occasions you both discussed, she has a history of deferring to Ray's wishes, even when it's not in her best interest. You worry that she will do the same with the inheritance.

Or say that you trust your son Harry fully. He's a good son and wise with his money. The problem, however, is that Harry married a spendthrift. His wife, Karen, likes to spend whatever is left over after the bills are paid. So far, Karen's and Harry's different financial habits haven't led to any problems in their relationship. Karen, while she likes to spend any extra money she earns, has always paid her share of the bills and spends equally on household needs. Still, you worry about giving Harry his inheritance outright because Karen might consider half of it hers and spend it on frivolous things.

If you want your child to fully share his or her inheritance with the spouse, by all means, give it as an outright bequest. If, however, you want your child to keep the inheritance separate, you should consider setting up protections that limit access to your child alone.

Whether or not you restrict your child's spending is up to you. If you think establishing the trust will create enough of a psychological barrier between your child's spouse and the money, you may not need to place any restrictions on how your child spends the money. Thus, it will be akin to an outright gift. If you're worried, on the other hand, that your child's spouse is savvy enough to know that he or she can demand equal say in how the trust money is spent, you might want to establish some controls—requiring, for example, that the money be saved only for emergencies or for your grandchildren's weddings or college education. This, of course, might offend your child or place him or her in a tough situation if the money is needed for a different purpose.

Establishing a trust for the purpose of keeping your child's inheritance away from his or her spouse is rife with possible uncomfortable outcomes. You need to decide whether protecting the money is worth offending your child and your child's spouse. Also, consider the potential furor that could befall your child after you die. Generally speaking, this is a wise tactic only if you seriously fear your child's spouse will misuse the money.

Look at it this way: By giving Harry the inheritance outright, you risk pitting him against Karen if he keeps the money for himself. If he chooses to share the money with her, you risk losing it to her frivolous spending habits. By putting the money in a trust, you become the bad guy, not Harry. If he chooses to let Karen spend the trust money on shoes, so be it. At least you attempted to give him a way out.

You can also serve another goal with a trust: You can ensure that any remaining assets are passed down to your grandchildren. Indeed, another danger of an outright inheritance is that your child's spouse can divert the money from your bloodline. Perhaps you trust your daughter and her husband to do the right thing with the money—namely, to spend it for the betterment of your grandchildren. What happens, however, if your daughter dies suddenly? It's likely that she will leave everything to your son-in-law, the father of her children. The inheritance would then become his to do with as he pleases. He could spend it on your grandchildren, as you and your daughter would have wanted—but it's his choice at this point.

PROTECTING THE INHERITANCE FOR THE NEXT GENERATION

Here's the dilemma for many people in a second or subsequent marriage: If you were to die first, your spouse would need your money to live on. Thus, you want to provide your spouse with access to your money for his or her life. You also want to make sure whatever is remaining goes to your intended beneficiaries, however, such as your kids from a first marriage.

Once you give an inheritance to someone outright, they can then leave it to whomever they want, regardless of your wishes. Your spouse might say that he or she will pass your house on to your children, but then decide to sell the house and keep the money. Even if you trust your spouse to give everything that remains of your estate to your intended heirs, life can thwart that plan. What happens if your spouse remarries and then dies before drafting a will that leaves your assets to your children? By law, your children's inheritance would be diverted to the new spouse.

Consider this hypothetical situation: Pierre and Chloe are both in their sixties, and both have been married before. Pierre has two children from two previous marriages. He owns his own house, worth about $350,000, plus he has about $650,000 in retirement funds and CDs. Chloe, a widow, has four children from her first marriage. She has savings worth about $250,000, most of which she obtained from the sale of her house when she married Pierre and moved in with him. If Pierre pre-deceases Chloe, he wants her to be able to live in his house until she dies, gets married, or moves into a nursing home. He also wants her to have access to his money so that she doesn't have to go back to work. He doesn't want to bequeath the house or his savings to Chloe, however, because he wants his children to be the ultimate beneficiaries.

If you want to ensure that your money stays in the family and is passed down to your bloodline only, consider an ongoing trust that will dictate not just who gets your money when you die, but also who gets whatever is left when your beneficiary dies.

Certain trusts can resolve this dilemma so that you don't have to choose between your spouse and your children. There are various types with many different names, including the so-called qualified terminal interest property (QTIP) trust, credit shelter trust, and bypass trust. To make this easier, let's take a closer look at the QTIP trust. With a QTIP, your money is placed in the trust when you die. You allow your spouse to have access to the income in the trust until he or she dies. Upon the surviving spouse's death, the trust money passes on to your ultimate beneficiaries, such as your children.

With a QTIP trust, the spouse has rights to the income, but you can also choose whether or not you want to provide him or her with access to the principal. If you do decide to allow your spouse to invade the principal, you can be very specific. He or she may have access to the principal at any time for any reason, or you might limit access to emergencies only—it's up to you. You can also make a provision that allows the principal to be tapped in case of a medical emergency, or only if your spouse has already depleted his or her savings. If this is the mother or father of your children (these types of trusts aren't just for second marriages), you may feel perfectly comfortable doing this. If this is a second marriage and your spouse and kids don't get along—you might want to limit access to the interest only. If you're worried that the interest from the trust won't be enough, consider giving an outright bequest of a smaller sum in addition to the trust.

You can name the spouse trustee, but whether or not you do this will depend on this spouse's relationship with your kids. If it's a second marriage and the new spouse doesn't get along with them, you may be setting yourself up for trouble. Your children may disapprove of the way your spouse is managing or spending the money, and whether or not there's any merit to such claims probably doesn't matter. Some of the biggest estate planning fights occur not between siblings, but between children from a first marriage and a second spouse, estate planners say.

PROTECTING YOUR SPECIAL-NEEDS CHILD

If you have a child (or any loved one) with a mental or physical disability, you face unique estate planning challenges. First, an outright gift may not be possible if the child lacks the mental ability to manage large amounts of money. An outright gift, or even an inheritance through an ongoing trust, can also cut your disabled child off from important government support.

Government programs, such as Supplemental Security Income (SSI) and Medicaid, are very important for people with disabilities since they can provide critical medical coverage and other support services. In order to qualify for these programs and benefits, however, the individual with the disability generally must have limited financial resources. Benefit recipients are generally allowed to have assets of no more than $2,000, with few exceptions. If you give your disabled son or daughter a big inheritance, you put your child at risk of losing Social Security and Medicaid services.

While you don't want to cut your child off from government

aid, you also don't want to leave him or her with nothing more than these programs, which tend to provide only for the bare necessities, such as food, shelter, and clothing. What about money for a vacation or for social events? How will your child pay for medical care or medications that aren't covered by Medicaid? What about money for an advocate to ensure your child is granted assistance by the government or money for a lawyer in case of legal problems?

If you leave the assets to someone else to care for your child, you risk losing that money if the caretaker is dishonest. Even an honest caretaker can lose the money if he or she runs into financial problems, including personal bankruptcy, lawsuits, a medical emergency, or unemployment.

The solution is known as a special-needs trust. This type of trust is designed specifically so that your child can take full advantage of government programs but still have money to use for extracurricular activities or for special purposes, such as a lawsuit. The key to a special-needs trust is that the money cannot be used for housing, food, or clothing. Those are considered "basic needs" under SSI and Medicaid laws. If the disabled person is receiving free housing, food, or clothing from someone else, including a family member or a trust, then the government benefits will be reduced or eliminated. Instead, the language of the trust will instruct the trustee to make payments only for other things, such as a vacation, a night out, or a lawyer or advocate in times of trouble.

Protecting the Inheritance from Creditors

Your heir doesn't have to be a credit card junkie to suddenly lose his or her inheritance to creditors. Any bout of hard luck, from unemployment to a medical mishap, can leave an inheritance in the hands of creditors. Lawsuits are another concern. In today's litigious society, a sizable legal judgment can be a bigger threat to an inheritance than financial bad luck or mismanagement. This is often a huge concern for parents with children in certain professions, such as doctors.

Spendthrift trusts can protect your child's inheritance from being lost to lawsuits or other creditors' claims. The level of protection this type of trust can provide, however, depends in part on the laws of the state where the trust resides and in the way the trust is structured. Generally speaking, the greater the discretion given to the trustee (who should not be the same person as the beneficiary), the greater the protection provided by the trust. Similarly, the less control provided the beneficiary, the greater the protection level for the assets in the trust.

The bottom line, however, is that such trusts aren't bulletproof. If a case is egregious enough, a court will often allow the trust assets to be accessed to pay off a lawsuit or a debt. Some states, for example, will allow trust assets to be breached to pay child support. Review these laws and past court cases before you rely on this method.

A family limited partnership (FLP) is another asset protection vehicle you might consider. With an FLP, you establish a limited partnership agreement and transfer the title of the property in question to the partnership. It's called a family limited partnership because it tends to be used by families. You and your spouse can be general partners, which means you can make all the decisions, and your children can be named limited partners. The benefits of FLPs are many, including probate avoidance and estate tax benefits. One of the greatest advantages of the FLP, however, is asset protection. If a creditor succeeds in a claim against a partner, the creditor will be assigned that partner's interest in the FLP. In other words, the creditor will have to stand around waiting for a distribution from the FLP rather than gaining access to the assets in the entity. Holding the partner's interest is no good, of course, if there are no distributions. Meanwhile, the creditor will be responsible for paying income taxes as a partner. In a nutshell, the creditor risks owing taxes but receiving no income, a position that would push any creditor to settle.

The limited liability company (LLC) is structured similarly to FLPs in many respects, but is often considered a less useful asset protection vehicle because the state laws governing LLCs vary widely. Before deciding between an FLP and an LLP, review your state's laws on these entities.

Meanwhile, there are major disadvantages to both strategies, so you want to do your research before you set up either structure. For one, the IRS has been closely scrutinizing FLPs in recent years, concerned that some have been structured solely for the purpose of evading taxes. If you want to set up an FLP, you have to have a legitimate business purpose. It cannot simply exist as a shell for you to shelter assets until you can distribute them to the partners.

WHEN IT COMES TO CONTROL, HOW MUCH IS TOO MUCH?

While there are many reasons to want to control the money you bequest to others, you want to be careful not to go too far. Rigid or inflexible plans can wind up hurting your heirs more than helping them.

The classic example is the mother who, convinced that education should be a priority for her daughter, writes a provision into a trust that her daughter should use the money to attend college. If she doesn't graduate within the designated time period, the money would then be distributed elsewhere, such as to charity. The mother dies while the daughter is on her way to graduating from college. Then disaster strikes. The daughter is hurt in a terrible accident and has to drop out of school. Her recovery takes a long time and pushes her graduation date past the time when her mother had expected her to finish. As such, she loses access to the inheritance, according to the terms of her mother's estate plan.

We all know that life can take many unexpected turns. You may want to protect against your addict son spending his inheritance on drugs, so you lock his inheritance away in a trust. What if, down the road, your son cleans up his act, gets a job, and starts a family? If you were alive, you might agree that he deserves complete access to his inheritance. If that money is locked away in a trust, however, this might be impossible.

Or perhaps you establish a trust to give your children their inheritance in increments starting when each one turns thirty-five because you believe most people aren't mature enough to handle large amounts of money before that age. What if, down the road, your twenty-nine-year-old archaeologist daughter gains the opportunity to work in Egypt on a special excavation project for a year, but she needs cash to support herself during that time? If you were alive, you would probably agree to give her the money. If the money is guided by strict trust instructions, however, the trustee might not be allowed to make any distributions before she turns thirty-five.

The point is, there are a number of reasons that you might want to change the terms of an ongoing trust down the road. When you're alive, you can decide when a situation warrants an exception to the rules. How do you deal with these situations when you're dead?

NAMING A TRUST PROTECTOR

Sometimes only changes to a trust document itself can address unforeseen circumstances, such as a change in the law that removes important protections for certain types of trusts, or changes in a beneficiary's financial circumstances that require an unusual payment. Typically, the trustee lacks the authority to make such changes. Enter the trust protector—a person you name to act as your voice from the grave, stepping in with the authority to impose major changes to the trust document as he or she sees fit to protect your beneficiaries.

Naming a trust protector shouldn't disrupt the day-to-day operations of the trust. Rather, the trustee will maintain the trust as expected, with the trust protector intervening only when he or she thinks it necessary for the benefit of the beneficiaries. The trust protector might, for example, determine that a formerly drug-addicted beneficiary has changed his ways and is ready for an outright inheritance, which would end the need for the trust.

Why might you want to name a trust protector in addition to a trustee? Generally, it's done in order to maintain both flexibility and control in a trust. Say you establish a trust to protect your spouse's inheritance, concerned that she's getting too old to manage her own accounts. You decide that management of the trust might be too much for your children, who live far away and have families of their own, so you hire a professional trustee. Still, you are worried that the professional trustee could neglect the needs of your spouse—or, even worse, take advantage of your spouse as she ages. In this case, consider naming one of your children trust protector, with authority to fire the trustee or require a detailed accounting of the trust at any time. The trust protector also has the authority to change investment advisers. This allows you the benefit of professional money management and distribution services with the added protection of a close family member to watch over the trust's administration.

A trust protector can also be helpful when the trustee is a family member. You may name your daughter as trustee of your spouse's inheritance, but still want an extra set of eyes watching to make sure she handles things appropriately.

What powers you give the trust protector will vary depending on your needs. Generally, the trust protector will have the right to fire the trustee, the investment adviser, or both, and to demand an accounting of the trust at any time. He or she may also have the power to add or delete beneficiaries, move the assets to a new trust, or terminate the trust and distribute the remaining trust assets to the beneficiaries. Just as with any position, be careful not to give the trust protector too much power—the idea is to provide a system of checks and balances. Only provide the trust protector with the powers you think are necessary to complete your wishes. You may want the trust protector to have the ability to terminate the trust if, for example, it was established to protect the inheritance of a drug-addicted child who you hope will one day kick the habit. On the other hand, you may not want to give the trust protector the ability to terminate the trust if doing so would result in adverse tax consequences.

TECH TALK: Be aware that some controls placed on an inheritance will not hold water in court, thus allowing the inheritance to pass along without conditions. The main rule is that the terms of an inheritance cannot go against public policy. You cannot, for example, set up a trust that requires your trustee or beneficiaries to use the money to support criminal or racist activities. Generally speaking, you also may not condition an inheritance upon religious faith or marriage. In other words, you cannot require that your son divorce his spouse and marry someone of your choosing in order to gain access to his inheritance. Still, this principle is open to some interpretation. Consider the case of David Shapira, MD,* who bequeathed part of his estate to his son, Daniel, on the condition that Daniel marry a Jewish girl, both of whose parents are also Jewish, within seven years of David's death. If, seven years later, Daniel had not carried through with his father's wishes, Daniel's share would go to the State of Israel. Daniel, twenty-one years old and unmarried, protested in court, arguing that the condition of his inheritance was against public policy and that he should be allowed to maintain the freedom to marry whomever he chose. You might assume Daniel's was an open-and-shut case. After all, the right to marry is protected by law. The courts, however, decided that the father's restraint on the choice of a marriage partner was not against public policy. Why? Well, Daniel still had the right to marry anyone he wanted—he just wouldn't receive his inheritance if he married against his father's wishes. The right to inheritance is not protected.

Shapira v. Union National Bank, 315 N.E. 2nd 825 (1974).

Chapter 11

PLANNING FOR PETS

Legally Speaking, Fido Is Property, Too

People with pets often assume that a family member or close friend will take on their companion animals when they die. In many cases, this would be true, especially when it's a shared pet—say, between a husband and wife. When one spouse dies, the other would automatically assume care for the pet. But this isn't true for all pet owners. And people who fail to plan for the worst may be placing their pets in a risky situation.

What Happens to Your Pet When Your Pet Outlives You?

If you have pets, you should understand the potential dangers that exist in not preparing for their care as part of your estate plan. According to the law, pets are nothing more than your property, not unlike a desk or a chair. So when you die, the heirs you've named to take your property would also inherit your pet. Whoever takes possession of your pet when you die becomes its new owner. The new owner has the right to do whatever he or she wants with it, including selling it, giving it away, or putting it in the pound. Even if the person who takes over the care of your pet wants to keep it, things can happen to thwart this goal. The new owner could move into an apartment with a strict no-pets policy, or start dating someone with pet allergies. How will the new owner react if your pet becomes very sick and the medical costs required to care for it become too much to bear? If you share your pet with, say, a spouse, you're probably less worried about these kinds of unexpected problems. What happens, however, if you and your spouse die simultaneously in a car accident?

There are many reasons why pet lovers might want to consider setting aside money for a pet and its new caregiver. This can be done through a will or a trust. Increasingly, pet lovers are also turning to institutions that, for a fee, agree to take care of people's pets for the rest of their lives. Here are some reasons you might want to consider more extensive estate planning for your pet:

- *You live alone:* If you live alone with a cat or dog, you need to ask yourself: *Who will take care of my pet when I die?* If you have no close family, you might be placing your pet at risk of going to the pound. You can always ask a friend to take it, but how certain can you be that this friend will still want it when you die? The pet could be old or sick by then, having lost the cute and cuddly appeal that attracts people to pets. What if the caregiver has kids who have developed pet allergies?

- *You have a costly or exotic pet:* If you are in this situation, you might also have a hard time finding someone to agree to be your pet's caretaker. Examples of costly or exotic pets can include snakes, big lizards, certain birds, horses, pigs, and monkeys. Even if your adult son would want your Savannah monitor (a reptile that has long claws and sharp teeth, and that can grow to be four feet long), would his wife approve? Even if your daughter would be willing to take your horse when you die, could she afford to feed it and keep it stabled?

• *You have many pets:* Your pet of choice may be the common household dog or cat, but if you have more than one, they could be too much for your loved ones to handle when you're gone. These days, it's not uncommon for people to have three or four dogs, or half a dozen cats—and they often want the animals to stay together for the rest of their lives. Even if you know someone who is willing to take your four dogs or three cats when you die, would that person have enough money to care for so many animals, especially as they age and require additional veterinary care?

• *Your pet is sick, or requires a lot of care:* As pets age, they can require a lot of costly and time-consuming care. Different pet owners handle this in different ways. Some will put their pets to sleep at the first sign of pain and suffering. Other pet owners will stop at nothing to provide the latest medical therapies. If your pet is sick and you believe in providing it with long-term care to keep it alive, you may have trouble finding someone to take it unless you provide funding for that purpose.

• *You don't know anyone who could meet your standards for care:* Even if your pet is healthy and appealing to everyone, you may provide it with extraordinary care that cannot be easily matched by anyone you know. Some people believe cats should be allowed to roam free outdoors; others are quite strict about never letting them go outside. Some people take their pets to the vet only when necessary and believe generic food is sufficient, while others demand regular checkups and special dietary supplements for their animals. If you are particular about your pet's care, consider planning for a caregiver who will live up to your standards. You also want to think about providing him or her with the money necessary to fund the cost of special foods and regular checkups.

Vickie fits into several of these groups. She is divorced with no children and four cats. Several of her cats are also sick and require expensive medical procedures. One of the cats, for example, sees a cardiologist every six months for an echocardiogram that costs roughly $350. Vickie has a friend who she feels will take good care of the cats if she dies, but she's concerned that her friend won't provide the same standard of care. In addition to the EKGs for the sick cat, Vickie provides her animals with regular teeth cleanings, blood work, and grooming—on top of their annual veterinarian visits. This can cost a lot of money, which Vickie is more than willing to shell out. The question is: Would her cats' new caretaker be willing to do the same?

A Pet Trust or Retirement Home?

How do you make sure Fido's needs are met by the new caretaker when you die? The first step is to name a caretaker and discuss your plans with this person. As with any other important position, you should also try to select a backup caregiver to take over if something happens to the first choice. Naturally, you want to choose someone you trust who also has some familiarity with your animal and experience caring for pets. Also, be sure to stay in touch. You want to be aware of any changes in your caregiver's personal circumstances that could affect his or her ability to care for your pet.

Next, consider setting aside money for the new caretaker to spend on your pet. This means calculating the cost of food, veterinarian exams, toys, and anything else you consider necessary.

If you have a horse, for example, think about the cost of keeping the animal stabled as well as veterinary bills.

Once you have done these two things, you can make your wishes known either through the will or in a trust. Each strategy has its own benefits and drawbacks.

- *The will:* A will is a fine strategy for people who have a trusted caretaker in mind, such as a spouse or adult child. Keep in mind, however, that you are essentially passing the pet on as property along with some money. As such, there is no way to ensure that the money you leave will be used for the care of the pet. Again, the pet is property in the eyes of the law. The new owner can spend the money on the property as you requested, or not.
- *The trust:* Historically, the law hasn't allowed people to establish trusts for their pets because a trust beneficiary had to be human. Laws are changing, however, and many states now allow residents to create trusts for the care of their pets. Some states even support enforcement of a trust on the pet's behalf. Before you establish a pet trust, be sure you know your state's laws. A court may, for example, be allowed to declare a trust excessive and reduce its funding. Your pet trust can become activated when you die or in the event that you become incapacitated and can no longer care for the animal. With a pet trust, you can be very specific about the care you want provided to your animal and what you want to happen to any remaining money after the pet dies.

TECH TALK: Although animals are considered property, there have been cases in which the courts have forbidden euthanizing pets, regardless of the wishes of the deceased. When Ida Capers died in the early 1960s, for example, her will requested that any dog she owned at the time of her death be destroyed in a humane manner. That meant the death of her two Irish setters, Brickland and Sunny Birch. The public outcry was so strong, however, that a number of politicians stepped in to advise the court to prevent the executor from carrying out the wishes of the deceased. Ultimately, the court agreed, and the animals were spared from following their mistress to the grave.

If you don't have anyone you trust to take your animal, consider an institutional caretaker, such as a pet retirement home or a no-kill shelter. Pet retirement homes, also known as pet sanctuaries, can come with a heavy price tag, but they promise to care for the pets left to them for life, including costly medical care. Others will take care of your animal for life only if attempts at placing them with a family fail. No-kill shelters agree to find your pet a home and promise not to kill the animal if they are unsuccessful.

Pet retirement homes are becoming popular because they eliminate the common concerns that come with individual caretakers—people become sick, they die, or they just don't want the pet anymore. These homes come in all shapes and sizes—and the cost can vary dramatically. Some are quite ritzy, offering orphan pets room and board in big houses with acres of yard for them to frolic in. There are also a number of simpler, mom-and-pop-type shops run by people—often couples—who simply want to devote their lives to homeless animals. Pet owners can also seek out retirement homes that specialize in unusual pets, such as exotic birds or potbellied pigs.

The Golden Years Retirement Home, which is owned by the Bide-A-Wee animal shelter, is a good example of a reasonably priced retirement home. The Westhampton, New York, sanctuary charges $10,000 per pet. It only accepts cats or dogs at least eight years old that have already been neutered, and that are free of any disease that might pose a threat to the other animals. In exchange, the center will care for the animals for their lives, including the cost of health care. It provides the animals with checkups every six months. It provides an exam room and a pharmacy on-site, and surgical and emergency facilities at the nearby Bide-A-Wee clinic. Pets live in dormitory-style accommodations that allow for socialization or privacy, whatever the pet chooses, as well as a full-time staff to play with the animals and meet their needs. The center even has a behaviorist to assess the animals' needs and communicate them to other employees. The dogs eat and sleep in large cubicles with soft bedding. During the day, they can play outside or frolic in the center's common area, chewing up furniture and watching doggy movies like *101 Dalmatians* with other orphaned dogs. The cats sleep in cubbies and play in a large room with cat toys, scratching posts, and climbing ledges.

How do people pay for this? One solution is that of Charlotte Reed—a small-business owner, pet consultant, and owner of a pet care shop in Manhattan—who has taken out life insurance policies to be paid to Bide-A-Wee's Golden Years Retirement Home in the event of her death. In exchange for the money, the home will care for her dogs until they die.

LOOK OUT! If you do choose a pet retirement home, make sure it has the financial means to survive as long as your pet does. Why? A quick look at the world of pet retirement homes reveals that many of them haven't been around that long. It's a bit of a fad to open a home for pets. And as we all know, fads pass. In fact, some pet retirement homes have signed contracts with pet owners but have yet to receive a single animal to care for. Others admit that they frequently accept animals for little or no charge because they feel sorry for them. Indeed, most pet retirement homes seem to have been established by well-intentioned people who love animals—but that's no guarantee that they will be around to care for your animal after you're gone.

Here's a look at some pet retirement homes and their costs:

• *Kansas State University's Perpetual Pet Care Program; perpetualpetcare@vet.k-state.edu, 785-532-4013:* Many pet sanctuaries and retirement homes are actually programs of veterinary schools. They are established to provide money to the school and access to animals for the students, who are often given charge of the animals in the program. The Perpetual Pet Program was established as a part of Kansas State University's college of veterinary medicine. The admission cost for a small animal is $25,000. Large animals cost $50,000, and admission for special-needs animals is $75,000. Attempts are made to put the animals up for adoption.

• *The Oasis Sanctuary; Oasis@the-oasis.org, 520-212-4737* is a retirement home strictly for exotic birds, including parrots, cockatoos, and macaws. The birds are not put up for adoption unless the sanctuary deems it necessary for an individual's well-being. The cost varies, depending on a multitude of factors, including the bird's life expectancy and medical needs.

• *The Best Friends Animal Society; info@bestfriends.org, 435-644-2001* is an animal sanctuary with an estate planning program that will care for up to six of your pets. Pets that cannot be placed in new permanent homes will be kept at the sanctuary for the rest of their natural lives. Certainly the price is right: People are asked to give as much as they can.

COMPILING INFORMATION ABOUT YOUR PET AND ITS CARE

One very important part of planning for your pet's care is to prepare written instructions for immediate care after you die or become incapacitated. Often, when someone dies, that person's home will be left to sit for quite a while—sometimes until well after the funeral, when the executor gets a chance to survey the property and the furniture. If you have pets, you need to ensure that someone knows they're there and can quickly step in to care for them in your absence.

The first step is to create an emergency card to carry in your purse or wallet that provides information about your pet, where it lives, and whom to contact to take care of the pet in your absence. It's not unlike a medical bracelet alerting medical personnel to important information even when you can't talk. In this case, however, the information concerns your helpless animal at home. The Placer Society for the Prevention of Cruelty to

Animals in Roseville, California, has prepared a typical emergency card:

Animal Care Card	Special Care Instructions: _____
In case of an emergency please ensure my pet is properly cared for.	_____ _____ _____ _____ _____
Name of pet: _____ Type of animal: _____ Location: _____ _____	
In an emergency please contact (name and phone number) for the temporary care of my pet: _____ _____	**Placer SPCA** 150 Corporation Yard Road Roseville, CA 95817 • 916-782-7722

In addition to the animal emergency card, you also want to provide written instructions about the care your animal requires for the person who comes to take care of your pet. Does the pet require any medications? Is it dangerous to other people? Who is the veterinarian and how do you contact him or her? If you have already designated a long-term caretaker, you should provide a copy of your care instructions to this person as well.

CHAPTER 12

PREPARING FOR INCAPACITY

THE NAME TERRI SCHIAVO SAYS IT ALL

Most of what I've discussed thus far—drafting a will, avoiding probate, creating trusts—assumes that death will happen suddenly. While we all hope that death takes us swiftly when it comes, this isn't always the case.

Indeed, there's always the possibility that you may enter a stage somewhere between life and death. You could be comatose or brain-dead. If a bus hits you tomorrow, for example, you may go into a coma or another incapacitated state before you die. Or you could come out of it all right. Nor is it just freak accidents that can push people into incapacity. As we age, we can lose understanding of what's going on around us and lose the ability to make sound decisions.

A good estate plan should plan for the possibility that you will enter just such a state. This is broadly termed *incapacity,* but it can mean many different things, from a temporary coma to permanent brain damage or even mental deterioration in old age.

The first reason you want to plan for incapacity is that you want to control your health care. With today's sophisticated medical technology, you could be kept alive despite physical damage that, in previous times, would have led to a certain death. Today people who cannot breathe or eat on their own can be kept alive through artificial means. This has led to many theological, political, and scientific debates over when life ends and when it begins. This book doesn't attempt to solve those debates. The point here is to warn you that however you feel about artificial life support should be reflected in your plan. Your family should know under what circumstances you want to be kept alive through any means necessary, as well as the point—if any—at which you want to be left to die.

Another reason to plan for incapacity is financial. If you're incapacitated, you want someone you trust to take over your finances for you. Also, incapacity, especially when it occurs in old age, can leave you vulnerable to financial abuse. Without a plan in place, you could be setting yourself up as a target for unscrupulous people and scam artists.

There are three main documents you want to consider drafting to protect you in case of incapacity:

- A living will.
- A health care power of attorney.
- A financial power of attorney.

TECH TALK: You may not need to hire a lawyer to draft these documents. Many states provide one or more of them free online, along with instructions on how to fill them out and rules governing their legality. The Arizona Secretary of State's Web site, for example, provides both living will and health care power of attorney documents. The Wisconsin Department of Health and Family Services' Web site offers forms for all three: a living will, a health care power of attorney, and a financial power of attorney. The New York Department of Health's Web site, meanwhile, provides a form for health care power of attorney, while the Iowa State Bar Association's Web site provides a living will template.

LIVING WILLS

Whereas a regular will allows you to speak from the grave, a so-called living will (not to be confused with a living trust) allows you to speak from the hospital bed in case of incapacity. This can be vital, because modern medical technology can keep people alive for a very long time, even when there's no chance their medical situation will ever improve. You may decide you want to be kept alive no matter what happens. Or you may prefer to move medical science aside and let nature take its course.

A living will allows you to clarify your wishes in just such a situation. A living will may also be called a health care directive, advance directive, or medical directive. You create one while you're healthy. It will become activated in the event of incapacity.

Keep in mind, however, that the living will is really only intended for critical situations—not for just any old hospital visit. It allows you to tell your health care providers and your family whether you want to pursue or withdraw life-sustaining treatment if you are on the verge of death or permanent incapacity—in other words, when there's little doubt that you will ever recover and the only question is whether you want modern medicine to prolong your life, or just to add some minimal comforts as you die.

It is recommended that you draft a health care power of attorney in addition to a living will so that you will have someone who can speak for you in situations that fall beyond the purview of the living will. Just because you're incapacitated doesn't mean your situation is irreversible. You want a health care guardian around in just such a case.

The first step to writing a living will is to seriously consider what kind of care you might want in a very dire medical situation when you couldn't speak for yourself. One of the main questions to ask yourself is: *Is there any medical situation I consider worse than death?* If the answer is no, then you know you want every treatment possible, and for as long as possible. If you decide you would rather die than live as a vegetable, consider requesting that life support be removed in case of brain damage.

Here are some more questions to ask:

- If you ever become terminally ill, how long would you want to be kept alive by artifical means?
- If you ever become unconscious and are unlikely to ever wake up, how long would you want to be kept artificially alive?
- If you are ever brain damaged or in a "persistent vegetative state," how long would you want to be kept artificially alive?
- How do you feel about resuscitation and surgery if you are ever in a state that is expected to lead to death?
- How do you feel about pain-relief medication, ventilators, and feeding tubes if you are ever in a state that is expected to lead to death?
- Would you want to be kept alive if you were in severe pain most or all of the time?
- Would you want to donate your organs or tissues after you die?

DICTIONARY

Terminology to Know When Drafting a Living Will

Terminal condition: An injury or illness that has no cure and from which there is no reasonable expectation for recovery even with medical treatment.

Persistent vegetative state: A condition in which a person loses the higher cerebral powers of the brain but maintains automatic activities, such as breathing, sleep and wake cycles, and eye movement. There is almost no chance of recovery for people who have been in such a state for more than one year.

Life-sustaining treatment: Generally, any medical intervention that prolongs the process of dying. It tends to include treatments such as feeding tubes and mechanical breathing devices, but can also include antibiotics and pain relief.

Do not resuscitate: A request to the hospital and other health care professionals that you do not want cardiopulmonary resuscitation, or CPR, if your heart stops or if you stop breathing. Unless given explicit orders to not perform CPR, hospital staff will try to help all patients whose heart has stopped or who have stopped breathing. People who might want to consider a DNR order are those who aren't likely to benefit from CPR. Generally, this includes people with kidney failure or severe pneumonia, and some terminal cancer patients. If you're considering a DNR order, be sure to discuss it with your doctor.

Remember to keep comfort in mind as well. Just because you don't want surgery or resuscitation doesn't mean you don't want food, water, or medication to relieve your pain. If you're unsure of what kind of situations might warrant direction from you in a living will, talk to your attorney and your doctor.

Once you know how you would want to be treated, you want to discuss your concerns with your family and your doctor. Family may not always support your wishes, but your doctor certainly should.

Next, draft a living will that expresses your wishes according to the laws of your state. Again, some states provide template forms that make this process easy. If so, you should be able to get ahold of your state's form from your local hospital, a doctor's office, a senior center, or an official state Web site. (For an example of a living will, see appendix 1.)

When writing a living will, be sure to keep your wishes simple and straightforward. If your wishes aren't immediately understandable, they may not be fulfilled. Another reason to keep things simple is because you cannot predict every possible medical situation that might arise. Again, your health care proxy should be able to deal with most issues, while your living will should be there simply to provide guidance about the most dire of situations.

Terri Schiavo: A Case Study

The name *Terri Schiavo* seems to say it all. For those not familiar with the case, Terri Schiavo was the Florida woman with severe brain damage who drew national media attention when, in 2005, the president of the United States and Congress stepped in with their opinions about whether she should be kept on life support—even passing a bill demanding that a federal court review her case.

Of course, Terri's battle with death had been going on long before 2005. Her struggle started in 1990, when she was just twenty-seven years old. She collapsed in her home after suffering cardiac arrest, leading to brain damage due to a lack of oxygen. Her husband, Michael, has said that his wife suffered from the eating disorder bulimia, which resulted in a potassium deficiency that triggered the heart failure. (An autopsy conducted after Terri's death found no evidence of an eating disorder. The autopsy supported Michael's contention that Terri was in a persistent vegetative state. She had irreversible brain damage and was blind.)

Terri hadn't prepared any written guidance about what kind of medical treatment she would want in case of incapacity; nor did she have any written statements about who should take control of her medical decisions if she couldn't do it herself. After she had been sent to the hospital, her husband, Michael, was appointed her guardian.

As early as 1993, her husband and her parents began to clash about what kind of treatment to give her. Terri's parents attempted to have Michael removed as Terri's guardian. In 1998, Michael petitioned the court to remove Terri's life support. Over the next seven years, the debate was brought before various courtrooms—all the way up to the U.S. Court of Appeals. In the end, Terri's feeding tubes were removed; she died thirteen days later, on March 31, 2005.

Had Terri provided her family with her wishes about life support in writing, the debate over whether she should continue life support would very likely have been resolved a long time ago. Her wishes would have been made clear to the courts. Instead, the courts had to rely on word of mouth from her husband, who said he'd discussed the topic with her when they were married, and the plaintive pleas of her then still-hopeful parents.

Regardless of where you stand on the Terri Schiavo case, it was plainly a terrible ordeal for her family and friends. Knowing what Terri wanted could have prevented much of this pain.

After you finish drafting your living will, make sure it becomes a part of your medical record. Also, see if you can submit a copy to your local hospital or nursing home. In addition, keep a copy for yourself and give one to your medical power of attorney.

TECH TALK: Michael Schiavo and the Money

Richard L. Pearse Jr. was appointed Terri's guardian in 1998, following Michael's petition to remove Terri's feeding tubes. In a report he submitted to the court later that year, he raised the question of the money that Michael stood to inherit if he was successful in his efforts to remove Terri's feeding tubes.

According to the report, Michael Schiavo pursued negligence litigation over Terri's medical treatment following her heart failure. The litigation resulted in a $750,000 award to Terri's estate. Michael was also awarded some money for his personal loss, paid in 1993.

There was no evidence that Michael ever misused Terri's funds, the report said. In fact, the money was placed in the custody of a bank that invested it in a diversified portfolio. By 1998, when the report was written, there was roughly $713,000 remaining in Terri's account.

Still, the report raised the money as a potential conflict of interest. Terri died without a will. So long as Michael remained her legal husband, he stood to inherit her entire estate under Florida's laws of intestate estates, according to the report. "Mr. Schiavo will realize a substantial and

---

fairly immediate financial gain if his application for with-drawal of life support is granted," the report said.

The point of this story isn't to cast doubt on Michael Schiavo. It's to demonstrate how sticky things can get when people fail to plan. If Michael Schiavo was, indeed, acting in his wife's best interest, he was unfairly criticized for carrying out her wishes and for accepting the money that she would have wanted him to have.

If he was acting in the interest of the money, Terri's life was potentially cut short before she would have wanted. Or perhaps it was a combination of both: Michael could have also acted in Terri's best interest re-garding her life support, but not so in accepting all her money. Perhaps she would have wanted some of it to go to her family or to charity. We will never know, because Terri had neither a will nor a living will.

HEALTH CARE POWERS OF ATTORNEY

In addition to drafting a living will, you also want to name someone you trust to speak for you from your hospital bed. To do this, you need to draft a health care power of attorney, which names a health care proxy, health care agent, or patient advocate. This is the person who speaks for you when you're incapacitated, directing your medical care, consulting with medical staff, and making decisions about treatment on your behalf. Your health care proxy would speak for you in case of any type of incapac-ity, not just the terminal or irreversible kind. By law, hospitals, doctors, and other health care providers generally must follow your proxy's decisions as if they were your own.

If you don't name a health care proxy, the court will do it for you. Some people name a proxy as a substitute for a living will, but this isn't wise. You want there to be no doubt that your proxy is acting in your best interest, and a living will can provide that kind of certainty. Family members who disagree with your proxy's decisions could try to get the proxy removed from your case. If you provide instructions about your care, either through a living will or in a proxy form, you can reduce the risk of doubts and disagreements among family and friends.

Signing a health care power of attorney and naming a proxy doesn't remove your right to make your own medical decisions. You still retain power over your medical care until your doctors determine that you are incapacitated and cannot make decisions on your own. At that point, your proxy will take over.

You can take steps to limit your health care proxy's authority if you want. You can usually do this by providing your agent with instructions to follow, either in your power-of-attorney form or in your living will. Otherwise, your agent will be allowed to make any health care decision on your behalf that you could have made had you been able to do so. Among your agent's powers: He or she can choose your treatments and withhold treatments. (Some states, however, don't allow an agent to withhold nutrition and hydration unless he or she has implicit directions from you that you would want it this way.) Be sure to read up on the laws of your state before naming a health care proxy. Generally, you will need witnesses, and none of them can be the person you named as your proxy. (For an example of a health care proxy document, see appendix 2.)

Here are some things to consider when selecting a health care proxy:

- Will this person be able to abide by your wishes and not act on his or her own emotions or beliefs?

- Will this person be able to stand up to unresponsive or obstructionist doctors or other medical staff?
- Will this person be able to stand up to family members who disagree with your wishes and want to impose their own decisions about your treatment?
- Can this person make responsible decisions about complex medical procedures?
- Does this person support your decisions regarding life support in case of severe incapacity or terminal illness?
- Is this person likely to be around when you will most need help?
- Does this person get along with the people in your family, or the people you care about most?

LOOK OUT! You generally cannot name your doctor or another health care provider as your medical power of attorney. These practitioners are viewed as having interests in your health care that may be contrary to your own. In New York, for example, if you select a doctor as your agent, he or she cannot simultaneously act as your attending physician.

FINANCIAL POWERS OF ATTORNEY

If you become incapacitated, you also want to make sure that someone is able to take control of your finances. Generally, this person is known as your attorney-in-fact. You can name an attorney-in-fact by signing a power of attorney granting him or her powers to transact business on your behalf.

There are generally three types of power of attorney:

• *Durable power of attorney:* If you sign a durable power-of-attorney document, you have essentially named someone to manage your finances right away. The powers are only revoked upon your command or your death.

• *Non-durable power of attorney:* A non-durable power-of-attorney document also goes into effect immediately. The powers cease, however, once you become incapacitated. This type of power of attorney is used for specific transactions, such as the closing on the sale of a residence or the management of someone's affairs while he or she is out of the country.

• *Springing power of attorney:* This gives someone the power to manage your finances only in some future time period, or based on some future event. Generally, people use it to cover incapacity. So once a doctor or two confirm that you cannot manage your own money, the power will "spring" into effect.

If your purpose is to plan for incapacity, you want to choose between a durable and a springing power of attorney. Springing powers sound great because they prevent your agent from gaining access to your money or property unless you cannot manage it yourself. This power does, however, come with certain drawbacks. Incapacity isn't always that easy to spot. Certainly if you are in a coma, there will be little debate that you cannot handle your own finances. When people lose control due to something as innocuous as old age, however, incapacity can be harder to prove. Also, your agent will have to go through the time-consuming process of gathering doctors' statements that demonstrate your incapacity. Plus, there are concerns that under the new privacy regulations imposed by the Health Insurance Portability and Accountability Act (HIPAA), some doctors may be reluctant to discuss a patient's medical records with anyone who is not the health care proxy. So even if you are incapacitated, your doctor may not be willing to provide evidence of that fact to your agent, thus preventing the springing powers from ever springing.

If you really trust your agent, you might as well create a durable power of attorney—just make it clear to that person that the powers should spring into effect only if you're ever incapacitated. If you don't trust your agent, well, you're in trouble no matter what you do.

You can also try naming more than one person to have power over your finances. In this case, be sure to specify whether your agents can act independently or if they must act jointly. If you decide that they have to act jointly, you are saying that they cannot make a move without the other's permission. The risk of this strategy is that it can result in a deadlocked estate if your agents fail to agree.

Regardless of the type of power of attorney you draft, your attorney-in-fact will have certain powers and responsibilities. You can authorize your attorney-in-fact to do any combination of the following:

- Write checks on your behalf from your checking account.
- Pay your bills and manage your expenses.
- Manage your banking accounts.
- Manage your properties.
- Buy or sell your properties.
- Manage your investment accounts.
- File your tax returns.
- Make legal claims and conduct litigation on your behalf.
- Make financial gifts on your behalf.
- Buy and sell insurance policies and annuities for you.
- Claim property you inherit.
- Collect income on your behalf, such as Social Security or pension distributions.
- Operate your business.

You want to decide for yourself what powers you think are necessary. Generally speaking, most attorneys-in-fact will be allowed access to banking accounts and other investments. They are also generally allowed to manage expenses, pay bills, and manage real estate. It's rarer, however, to give someone authority to make financial gifts (although more estate planners recommend that this power be added for people who may be subject to estate taxes, because you can potentially lower your bill by giving assets away during life). If you're planning for incapacity, you want to be sure to give your agent the ability and funds to manage your expenses and your property, to collect your income, and to pay your bills, at the very least.

If you own everything jointly with someone, such as a spouse, you may still want a power of attorney. This is because your partner can generally manage money in a jointly owned bank account without your permission, but he or she will probably have less room to maneuver when it comes to jointly owned stocks or jointly owned real estate. If you have property in a living will, your successor trustee will be allowed to take control of the trust and the property and assets in the trust in case of your incapacity. Having a power of attorney won't affect this process. Having a living trust, however, doesn't negate your need for a power of attorney—you still need someone to take charge of assets outside the living trust and any income you receive from pensions or other sources. Plus, your power-of-attorney agent will be able to pay your bills.

FIGHT ELDER ABUSE BEFORE IT'S TOO LATE

One very good reason to have power-of-attorney protection in place is elder abuse. *Elder abuse* is a relatively new term to describe an age-old practice: the abuse, neglect, and exploitation of people who have become vulnerable due to aging. Many cases of elder abuse don't involve money. Older people can be harmed physically, sexually, and emotionally without finances becoming involved. Still, greed is definitely one of the main drivers of elder abuse, leading to financial exploitation.

Despite the fact that abuse of people who have become weak due to their age has been around forever, research on it is still in its infancy. What is known is that the perpetrator can be anyone, including strangers, hired caretakers, or even trusted financial advisers. Most perpetrators, however, tend to be loved ones. Indeed, more than 60 percent of the perpetrators reported for elder abuse were family members, according to a 2000 study conducted by the National Center on Elder Abuse.* Thirty percent were spouses or intimate partners, and 17 percent were adult children.

With people living longer than ever, there's concern that elder abuse could become an even bigger issue in the near future. If you think it isn't a problem now, just take a closer look at the news. Reports show that anyone can become a victim, including powerful people who were once very much in control of their lives.

The story of Babette Holmes, as reported by the *Sarasota Herald-Tribune*,** is quite jarring. Mrs. Holmes, granddaughter of one of the founders of the Fleischmann's margarine company, was reportedly victimized by Terrance McDonough, a maître d' she had befriended at a local country club in the early 1980s. Although Mr. McDonough was more than thirty years her junior, Mrs. Holmes took a liking to the fellow and showered him with gifts and money for many years. She bailed him out of jail in 1989,

---

*"A Response to the Abuse of Vulnerable Adults: The 2000 Survey of State Adult Protective Services," conducted by the National Association of Adult Protective Services Administrators (NAAPSA) for the National Center on Elder Abuse (NCEA).

**"A Matter of Trust: The Long Legal Struggle Over One Woman's Money and Independence," *Sarasota Herald-Tribune,* May 18, 2003.

for example, and loaned him money to keep afloat a sinking business venture he started in 1987. Mrs. Holmes even wrote Mr. McDonough into her will, leaving him 20 percent of her estate.

The situation got sticky in 1999, when the elderly woman went to the hospital following a bad fall. Mr. McDonough reportedly went to the hospital to visit the sickly woman about a week after she was admitted. That day, she also reportedly signed documents removing her Connecticut financial adviser as the co-trustee to her trust, leaving herself as sole trustee. She was in bad health and could barely muster a signature, even misspelling her name more than once, according to the news story.

Her former trustee alerted authorities of his suspicion that Mrs. Holmes was in trouble. The state quickly intervened and appointed a temporary guardian for her. The police also started an investigation. In late 2002, Mr. McDonough was arrested on charges of elder exploitation and grand theft. As of this writing, the case against Mr. McDonough was still pending, and he had not been convicted of any wrongdoing. Still, the ordeal has already put Mrs. Holmes through a long and costly court battle over her capacity. A judge determined in 2002 that Mrs. Holmes was partially incapacitated and appointed a third-party attorney to handle her money. As the *Sarasota Herald-Tribune* put it: "There were lawyers fighting for and against having the court name a guardian to handle Holmes' affairs, and she was paying all of them."

Mrs. Holmes had created a form of protection by naming a co-trustee to her trust. The financial adviser was responsible for her finances, but she could step in at any time and take over. When she signed paperwork to make herself sole trustee, the former co-trustee knew something was wrong and alerted the authorities. Of course, this method proved to be far from foolproof. The co-trustee in Mrs. Holmes's case lived in a separate state and seemed not to have been aware of any wrongdoing until he was cut out of the picture.

Another possible solution would be to name a trust protector. The trust protector carries no day-to-day fiduciary or administrative duties. This person is responsible for making sure that everything is running smoothly and has the power to implement changes as he or she sees fit. The role of a trust protector is akin to a board of directors for a corporation: to maintain a system of checks and balance. (Learn more about trust protectors in chapter 10.)

Of course, the usefulness of many of these tools really depends on whom you choose to fill the role of protector, co-trustee, or attorney-in-fact (the person with power of attorney). If the person you choose to watch over you and your spouse isn't trustworthy, putting that person in charge would be like giving a burglar keys to your vault.

This seems to have been the concern of a woman from Maine, whom I'll call Betty, according to a 2004 court complaint filed by Betty. Her daughter was brought to Maine to protect her after her husband died. Instead, the daughter spent Betty's money and tried to evict her from her own home, Betty said.

In 2002, Betty's husband found out he had terminal cancer and was given less than two years to live. Upon hearing the news, the couple decided to transfer partial ownership of their house to their daughter, assuming this would protect them from losing the house to medical bills. They informed their daughter of their plan and told her that it was on the condition that she move to Maine and take care of her mother after her father died.

After Betty's husband died, her daughter indeed moved to Maine to take care of her mother. Betty even gave her daughter control of her checking and savings accounts so that she could manage the household expenses, according to the court claim Betty later filed. Although the daughter had legal rights to the property, Betty considered it her own and continued to assume the financial burden, including property taxes and improvements.

After a while, Betty started to feel unwanted. Her daughter's boyfriend moved in and was watching her movements, she said in the complaint. Once, he even played back a recording he had made of her without her prior consent or knowledge. Betty moved out of the house into a ceramics shop on the same premises six months after her husband died. The shop was separate from the house and had neither a shower nor a kitchen, according to the filing.

About a year later, Betty was hospitalized. During this time, her daughter changed the locks on the house to prevent her mother from entering the premises and threatened to evict her if she returned, Betty alleged. That's about the time Betty decided to take action in the courts.

Betty's story is frightening for many reasons. She felt like a prisoner in her own home, and the one person she was relying on to take care of her in her old age was the very person who, she feared, was taking advantage of her frailty. What good is a power of attorney or any other protection if the person given control will abuse it? Truth be told, such protections can be a double-edged sword. An attorney-in-fact can be a savior to an incapacitated person or a nightmare if he or she takes advantage of the power.

In addition to an attorney-in-fact, you want to have a good network of people around you, according to people who have dealt with elder abuse cases. When you are relying solely on one person for everything, there's a greater chance that no one will notice if that person has turned against you. If you keep in touch with your friends, your doctor, and as many relatives as possible, you increase the chances that someone will notice if things go awry.

CHAPTER 13

UNMARRIED COUPLES

NOT PLANNING IS NOT AN OPTION

If you have a partner, but you're not legally married, not planning is not an option. Why? Well, a married couple can at least fall back on their right of election or their share of the community property. Unmarried couples are essentially strangers to one another in the eyes of the government, regardless of how many years they may have been living together and commingling assets.

Some states continue to enforce the idea of the common law marriage, or unions between couples who act married but never formally tie the knot. Still, the number of states that recognize such marriages is decreasing. A number of states that once recognized common law marriages have since abolished those laws by statute. Idaho, Georgia, and Ohio, for example, stopped recognizing common law marriages in the 1990s, and now recognize only those created before the year in which such laws were abolished.

For unmarried couples, estate planning has to be thorough and precise. Any mistake can leave your partner out in the cold. Consider Amy's story. Her boyfriend of twenty years wrote a will leaving everything to her. The problem was that he didn't follow proper procedure when writing his will. If you read chapter 2, you know that you cannot allow any of your beneficiaries to also act as witnesses to the signing of your will. Unfortunately, neither Amy nor her boyfriend knew about this seemingly minor regulation. After Amy's boyfriend completed his will, he had Amy act as one of the witnesses. In addition, the other witness signed the will on a different day, also procedurally incorrect.

When Amy's boyfriend died, his will was invalidated. Because the two were never married, Amy was left with nothing. According to the law of an intestate estate, all the assets and property were transferred to the boyfriend's closest living relative.

WHAT'S DIFFERENT FOR UNMARRIED COUPLES?

Here are some of the planning considerations for unmarried couples:

- *Domestic partnership agreement:* This is essentially a prenuptial agreement without the nuptials. It's a contract that outlines the legal rights and responsibilities of each partner, used when a couple decides to form a long-term committed relationship. Marriage is also a form of contract, bound by the rules established by the government. With a domestic partnership agreement, you get to set your own terms. In the event of a dispute, the domestic partnership agreement can help clarify ownership of property. In the event of a separation, it will provide guidance for dividing the property. Without this document in place, there's no claim to assets that aren't in your name. So even if both partners contributed financially to a house, only the legal owner would have claim to it in a separation.

• *Health care power of attorney:* As stated in chapter 12, everyone should have a health care power of attorney so that someone can manage your care in case of incapacity. This is especially important, however, for unmarried couples. Why? Well, if you fail to name a health care proxy, the court will have to step in and name someone. If you're married, the court will most likely name your spouse, assuming he or she is willing and able. If you're not married, however, the court may be more willing to choose your brother or mom over your partner. A health care power of attorney is also vital in case of an accident. When someone is admitted to the hospital, only close family is allowed visitation rights. If you're not married, you're not family. Technically speaking, the hospital can shut you out from seeing your partner. It can also refuse to answer your questions about what is happening to him or her.

• *Will or living trust:* It's imperative that unmarried couples draft a legal document guiding their wealth transfers after death. This means drafting a will, a living trust, or both. If you die without a legal will or trust, your estate will be transferred intestate, or according to the rules of the state. Everything you own will automatically go to your closest of kin, usually parents first and then siblings, in the absence of a spouse and children.

• *Power of attorney:* Also discussed in chapter 12 is the importance of power of attorney in case of incapacity. Again, this document names someone to manage your financial decisions for you in case you can't. You may not want to choose your partner to take on this role. If you don't choose your partner, however, you want to make certain that the person you choose is sensitive to the needs of your partner and will take care of him or her in your absence.

• *Beneficiary designations:* These documents determine who gets assets such as life insurance, IRAs, 401(k)s, and savings accounts in case of your death. If you don't fill these out, the assets generally go directly to blood relatives in the absence of a spouse.

• *Insurance:* Unmarried couples generally need a lot more insurance to protect against one partner's death because they can't count on receiving the partner's benefits, such as Social Security or pension distributions. If your estate is large enough to owe estate taxes, you definitely want to consider more life insurance to pay off this tax bill. Why? Only married couples can benefit from the marriage deduction, which allows an unlimited amount of money to pass to a spouse free of estate taxes. If you're not married, any money you transfer to your partner above the exclusion amount will be taxed.

SAME-SEX COUPLES MUST GRAPPLE WITH DIFFERING LAWS

Traditionally, same-sex couples have been at a particular disadvantage because they could not get married even if they wanted to. Moreover, they often face resistance from family members who object to their lifestyle, raising the issue of will contests and other problems after death.

While this is still the case in most parts of the country, things are changing. Some states, including Vermont and California, are beginning to acknowledge same-sex partnerships, giving them inheritance rights similar or equal to those of married couples. Massachusetts, meanwhile, recently became the first state to allow full-fledged marriage rights for same-sex partners.

If you live in a state that recognizes same-sex unions or same-sex marriage and you take advantage of those laws to create a legal union with your partner, you may think you're safe from many of the estate planning problems of unmarried couples. Instead, you may be facing even more problems than if you had never gotten married. Differing state and federal laws actually create a more complex set of planning problems for same-sex couples, who now need to grapple with multiple sets of different rules.

One reason is that the federal government won't recognize a same-sex marriage or civil union as long as the Defense of Marriage Act (DOMA) remains in effect. This act, signed by President Clinton in 1996, ensures that for federal purposes, marriage is defined solely as a union between a man and a woman.

Since the federal government won't recognize your union, neither you nor your partner will benefit from any of the federal perks for married couples. Here are some of the benefits lost under DOMA to couples who are otherwise joined under the rules of their state:

- *Marital deduction:* If you're married, you can transfer an unlimited amount of money at death to your spouse free of estate tax consequences—a benefit known as the marital deduction. A same-sex couple married by the law of Massachusetts will benefit from the marital deduction at the state level, but not at the federal. So the federal government will tax any money transferred to a spouse above the personal exemption amount.
- *Gifts:* The same holds true for gifts. The federal government tracks and taxes large financial gifts in order to prevent people from whittling down their assets ahead of death and, therefore, avoiding having to pay an estate tax. If you're married, you can give away unlimited amounts of money and property to your spouse without triggering a gift tax. If you're not married, any amount you transfer to your partner

above $12,000 a year will require you to file a federal gift tax return. Say you assist your significant other with the mortgage payments to the tune of $13,000 a year. The extra $1,000 will be considered a taxable gift for same-sex couples, even those who are legally joined by the laws of their state.

• *IRA rollover:* Federal laws allow a surviving spouse to "roll over" a deceased spouse's IRA or other qualified retirement plan account into a new IRA. Under DOMA, a same-sex married couple in Massachusetts would not be allowed to benefit from this rule.

• *Social Security:* Nor can your partner benefit from other types of federal programs when you die, such as the transfer of Social Security benefits.

Meanwhile, what happens if you live in a state that doesn't recognize same-sex unions? Suddenly, all your rights fly out the window. While a handful of states have enacted rules recognizing same-sex unions, dozens have passed legislation that defines marriage as being between a man and a woman. So a marriage license in Massachusetts may mean nothing if you move to Minnesota or Alaska, where your partner can still be cut off without legally binding instructions from you that direct otherwise.

Consider: You live in Massachusetts and are legally married to your partner because that state recognizes same-sex marriage. As such, you feel it's not necessary to create a health care power of attorney. You figure that if you're ever hospitalized, your partner will have visitation rights because you're married. If you ever become incapacitated, your partner plans to seek legal guardianship, and vice versa. Sounds like a decent plan, no? Well, what happens if, while on vacation in sunny Florida, you fall off your surfboard and become unconscious? You will be admitted to a hospital in Florida, a state that doesn't recognize same-sex unions. Without a legal health care power of attorney, your partner could technically be shut out of the decision making.

Or consider this: Say you're married in a state that recognizes same-sex unions and you draft a will accordingly. Years later, you buy a property in Alaska because you and your partner enjoy the vigorous outdoor activities available there. Without an updated will, that property will go directly to your blood relatives when you die, as Alaska doesn't recognize same-sex partnerships.

Even if you live in a state that recognizes same-sex unions, you cannot avoid planning. State rules relating to same-sex marriages are unstable at best, and can change just as swiftly as they arrive. Hawaii's Supreme Court, for example, determined several years ago that denying same-sex couples access to marriage licenses was against the state's constitution, the same as Massachusetts's 2003 Supreme Court ruling. A year later, Hawaii's legislature amended the state marriage laws to define marriage as a union between a man and a woman. Currently, same-sex couples who are residents of Hawaii can register as reciprocal beneficiaries but cannot be married.

CHAPTER 14

TAXES

ASSUMING YOUR HEIRS WON'T BE
TAXED IS THE FIRST MISTAKE

Estate taxes are for the rich, right? Generally speaking this is true, but don't be foolish enough to assume that it's always the case.

It's easy to see why people might think estate taxes are only for the rich. Over the next few years, the federal government will allow people to shelter more from estate taxation than ever before. Consider: If you died in 2001, you would have been taxed for transferring amounts more than $675,000 to your non-spousal heirs. In 2006, the exemption amount is $2 million. By 2009, you will be allowed to transfer $3.5 million to non-spousal heirs free of federal taxes, and in 2010 the estate tax will be repealed, giving you one year to transfer as much as you want to whomever you want free of taxation.

That's a lot of money to pass on tax-free. Yet you don't want to shrug off too quickly the possibility that you will be subject to estate taxes. It's possible for people with $1 million or less to get

Post–2001 Tax Act (new system)			Pre–2001 Tax Act (old system)		
Year	Estate Tax Exemption	Top Rate	Year	Estate Tax Exemption	Top Rate
2001	$675,000	55%	2001	$675,000	55%
2002	$1 million	50%	2002	$700,000	55%
2003	$1 million	49%	2003	$700,000	55%
2004	$1.5 million	48%	2004	$850,000	55%
2005	$1.5 million	47%	2005	$950,000	55%
2006	$2 million	46%	2006	$1 million	55%
2007	$2 million	45%	2007	$1 million	55%
2008	$2 million	45%	2008	$1 million	55%
2009	$3.5 million	45%	2009	$1 million	55%
2010	Tax repealed	Tax repealed	2010	$1 million	55%
2011	$1 million	55%	2011	$1 million	55%

snagged without proper planning. State estate taxes, for example, can snag estates worth $1 million and less. Meanwhile, the exemption amount will fall back to $1 million in 2011 unless the laws are changed before then. Also, the inheritance tax can present additional costs for heirs.

Consider the following hypothetical scenario: Tony is a single guy who lives in New Jersey. He's well off, but not what you would call rich. He owns a home worth roughly $400,000 in an upscale New Jersey suburb, and he has roughly the same amount saved up in his retirement fund, which he doesn't touch because he lives off his plush government pension and Social Security. Tony is divorced and currently lives with his girlfriend, Tina. He also has a teenage daughter. When Tony dies, all of his assets will be placed in a type of trust that will allow his girlfriend to live off the income until she either dies or gets married. At that point, the assets in the trust will be passed on to Tony's daughter. Tony has also given Tina the right to live in his home until she dies, gets married, or moves to another home for any period longer than six months. The property will then pass on to his daughter.

Tony is pretty savvy, so he knows his $800,000 estate won't be subject to federal estate taxes, which have been rising steadily in recent years. He has read several times in the paper that the death tax exemption will rise to $3.5 million in 2009. By 2010, the whole tax will disappear, leaving people to pass on as much as they want for one year. When the estate tax returns in 2011, the government will only tax estates worth more than $1 million.

What Tony doesn't realize, however, is that New Jersey has recently implemented its own estate tax, which taxes non-spousal death transfers of $675,000 and up. Were Tony and Tina married, he would avoid the state's estate tax. Under the circumstances, however, Tony's estate will be hit up for a state tax on roughly $125,000. Furthermore, Tony's beneficiaries are subject to the state's inheritance tax.

While the estate tax hits the estate, the inheritance tax charges heirs directly. The inheritance tax is generally implemented on a sliding scale, with the tax levies rising for beneficiaries who are not directly related to the deceased. In this case, Tina will have to pay a tax of 15 percent on the first $700,000 and 16 percent on anything above that amount.

The point is: You can't just assume your heirs won't be affected by taxes when you die. While the vast majority of Americans escape estate taxation, it's not impossible for average Americans to be hit. This isn't to say you want to obsess over this potential problem, especially if you don't have a lot of money. Only a few states tax estates worth $1 million or less. Still, it is something to consider when working on your inheritance plan.

CALCULATING YOUR RISK

When it comes to estate taxes, there are three main questions you want to answer to determine whether or not your estate will be taxed.

How Big Is Your Taxable Estate?

Your taxable estate involves anything of value that you plan to transfer to people after you die. This includes real estate, retirement savings, bank accounts, insurance proceeds, and certificates of deposit. It can also include personal items of value, such as paintings, jewelry, and some furniture.

What Kind of Deductions and Exemptions Might You Take?

After you have calculated your taxable estate, you want to consider what deductions and exemptions you might be able to take to reduce the amount that's taxed. There are roughly three major types of deductions and exemptions:

- *The marital deduction* is a great tool, and helps a lot of people who might otherwise be taxed escape taxation. Basically, any money or property a deceased person leaves to a surviving spouse, no matter how great the value, is exempt from taxation. (Different rules apply to non-citizen spouses.)
- *The charitable deduction* exempts from taxes all property and assets left to a tax-exempt charity.
- *The personal exemption* is the amount the government says you can automatically shelter from taxes when you die. The problem with this exemption is that it's changing fast. It started out at $1 million in 2002 and hits $2 million in 2006, where it stays for three years until 2009. It rises to $3.5 million in 2009 before returning to $1 million in 2011. This changing exemption amount can make it difficult for people

to plan. A single woman with an estate worth $1.5 million, for example, could get off scot-free if she dies anytime between 2006 and 2009 (also 2010 when the estate tax disappears). Should she die in 2011, however, she suddenly faces the risk of taxation. If this seems shockingly capricious, many legislators think it is, too, so changes may be afoot.

How Do State Estate Taxes Fit into the Computation?

Once you have computed what you might owe on the federal side, you then must assess what impact, if any, state estate taxes might have on your estate. Unfortunately, each state has its own rules on this matter. Plus, those rules are rapidly changing as states struggle to keep up with the changes in the federal rules. Some, such as Florida, currently charge no state estate tax because their estate tax system is linked to the federal government, which has eliminated subsidies to states for estate tax; others tax non-spousal transfers of just $675,000. Additionally, some states charge an inheritance tax, or a tax to the beneficiary based on the amount that was inherited and the relationship of the beneficiary to the deceased.

A Case Study: Ron

For a better understanding of how you might compute your potential tax liability, let's take a look at Ron—a fabricated character—and his various options. Ron lives in Boston with his wife. He owns two houses—one in the city and one near the beach. Together, his real estate holdings are worth about $600,000. Plus, Ron has accumulated savings worth roughly $900,000 over his lifetime, leaving him with a combined estate worth about $1.5 million.

When Ron dies, he faces several tax possibilities. What he will owe, if anything, depends largely on who gets his money and the year in which he dies. Let's first assume that Ron dies in 2009, leaving his wife and three kids behind. The federal estate tax exemption that year will rise to a high of $3.5 million. Meanwhile, the Massachusetts estate tax exemption will remain steady at just $1 million.

No matter who gets his money, Ron's beneficiaries don't need to worry that the estate will trigger a federal estate tax. Why? Well his $1.5 million estate falls well below the $3.5 million exemption amount. Ron may, however, have to pay something to the state since his estate is worth $500,000 over the $1 million exemption amount. Whether or not he will trigger a state estate tax, however, depends largely on who gets his property.

First, let's assume that Ron plans to give his primary home and half of his savings to his wife for a total transfer worth $850,000. That entire amount will qualify for the Massachusetts state marital deduction. As such, he technically has only $650,000 worth of property to leave to his children, all of which falls under the state exemption amount of $1 million. Thus Ron doesn't owe a dime in estate taxes to either the federal government or the state of Massachusetts.

There are other scenarios that might occur, however, that would leave Ron with a taxable estate. Ron may decide to leave everything to his children. If his wife agrees with this decision (in other words, she doesn't go after her rightful spousal share), he would owe tax money to the state. Why? He would be taxed on any transfer above $1 million to non-spousal heirs. In this case, the transfer of $1.5 million to his kids would trigger taxation on $500,000.

Meanwhile, if Ron left everything to his kids but died in 2011 rather than in 2009, he would have to worry about both federal and state estate taxes since the federal estate tax exemption is scheduled to drop to $1 million that year.

On the other hand, if Ron lived in Florida or Nevada instead of Massachusetts, he wouldn't have to worry about state estate taxes at all (at least until 2011) since neither of those two states currently charges a separate estate tax.

TECH TALK: Why So Many Different State Laws on Death Taxes?

If you're not up-to-date with your state's rules on estate taxes, don't feel bad. The phenomenon of states charging a separate estate tax is a pretty recent one, triggered by massive changes to the tax code passed in 2001.

Prior to that year, state death taxes generally were not a problem—no matter how wealthy you were. That's because most states relied on the federal government to pay their residents' estate tax bills through a system of dollar-for-dollar tax credits, up to a certain limit. To avoid burdening residents with state death taxes, most states charged only as much as the federal government was willing to pay in the form of subsidies, allowing states to fill their coffers with estate tax dollars without imposing a real tax on taxpayers.

The 2001 tax act changed all that because it repealed those credits—reducing them by 25 percent a year starting in 2002 until they disappeared entirely in 2005. States that were basing their estate taxes on the amount of credits that residents might get back suddenly found themselves getting less and less. In 2005, states that remained tied to the federal system of credits, such as Florida, effectively lost this stream of revenue.

This left states with two options: Either remain tied to the federal system of credits and lose estate tax revenues, or separate from the system, impose a real estate tax, and risk pushing wealthy residents away.

By 2004, the year before the credits were set to expire, seventeen states and the District of Columbia had separated from the federal tax system in a process known as decoupling. Every state implemented its own rules. Some states, such as New Jersey and Wisconsin, set their exemption amounts at a mere $675,000. Others linked their exemptions to the pre-2001 tax rules, meaning that residents can exempt $1 million from state estate taxes starting in 2006.

It's certainly been a topic of debate in many states. Pennsylvania, for example, decoupled in 2002, only to recouple again the next year. Meanwhile, states that remain decoupled continue to debate the issue.

TYPES OF TAXES THAT CAN AFFECT YOUR PLAN

The Inheritance Tax

In addition to estate taxes, a number of states also impose what's known as an inheritance tax. This is slightly different from the estate tax in that it's imposed on property the beneficiary receives. The heir or beneficiary pays the inheritance tax. The estate tax, on the other hand, is the tax imposed for the right to transfer property, and the estate pays this tax, not the beneficiaries. (Of course, beneficiaries can be hurt by estate taxes when they have to sell valuable assets, such as a home, in order to pay the tax bill. Plus, estate taxes can lower their ultimate inheritance.)

Another thing that makes the inheritance tax quirky is that the tax levied is based on the beneficiaries' relationship to the deceased. Spouses and direct descendants, such as children, are often exempt. Closer relations, such as brothers and sisters, may be taxed at a lower rate than cousins or nieces and nephews. Meanwhile, friends and non-spousal mates will generally be taxed at the highest rates.

Iowa, for example, separates beneficiaries into four classes. The first class, which consists of spouses, can inherit all they want free of the state's inheritance tax. The second class, which includes parents and children, is subject to taxation from 1 percent for an inheritance of up to $5,000, up to 8 percent for an inheritance of $150,000 and over. The third class of heirs includes siblings and sons- or daughters-in-law. This group is taxed at 5 percent for inheritances up to $12,500 and up to 10 percent for gifts of $150,000 and over. Everyone else is taxed 10 percent for inheritances worth up to $50,000 and up to 15 percent for gifts of $100,000 and over.

Gift Taxes

When learning about estate taxes for the first time, a lot of people think: *Estate taxes? Phooey! I'll just give it all away before I die. That way, there will be nothing left to tax!* If this thought has crossed your mind, you get points for creativity, but none for proper estate planning. The federal government is at least one step ahead of you.

In order to prevent people from escaping estate taxation by whittling away their assets before they die, the federal government has instituted what's known as a gift tax. The gift tax, as its name suggests, taxes large wealth transfers, or gifts, made during life. (It's a tax on the giver of the gift, not the recipient.)

Don't fret, not all gifts are taxable—your birthday and Christmas presents are probably safe from taxation. Indeed, much like the death tax, there are several exceptions to the rule, known as exclusions. Knowing what kind of wealth transfers will trigger the gift tax is important because proper gifting can reduce your risk of having to pay an estate tax. Improper gifting, on the other hand, can lead to an unwanted tax bill.

The exclusions to the gift tax rules are as follows: You can give away as much as $12,000 per person per year to as many individuals as you want. Each spouse has this right so, combined, a husband-and-wife team can give away $24,000 per person per year. A couple with five kids, therefore, can technically hand over $120,000 to their kids in one year totally free of IRS scrutiny.

Other exceptions include spouses and charity. You can give away unlimited amounts to your spouse or to a tax-exempt charity and the IRS won't blink an eye. You can also give unlimited amounts to political organizations without incurring a gift tax. Plus, you can give away unlimited amounts toward a person's medical expenses or tuition. This means you can pay for your grandson's college tuition, pay for his knee surgery (injuries from soccer practice), and still give him $12,000 for spending money in one year—all free of gift taxes.

So far, that's six exceptions to the rule. Let's review them:

- $12,000 per person, per year.
- Unlimited amounts to a spouse.
- Unlimited amounts to charity.
- Unlimited amounts to a person's medical expenses.
- Unlimited amounts to a person's tuition.
- Unlimited amounts to political organizations (gee, wonder who thought of that?).

TECH TALK: To qualify for the unlimited exclusion for qualified education expenses, you must make your payments directly to the educational institution and for tuition only. If you give the money to the student, it won't count as part of the unlimited tuition exclusion, but rather as an outright gift. Payments made for school supplies and living expenses, such as books, don't qualify for the unlimited exclusion.

Also, contributions to so-called qualified state tuition programs don't qualify for the unlimited tuition gift tax exclusion. A qualified state tuition program is any program sponsored by states or educational institutions that allows people to pre-pay tuition or contribute to an account established for that purpose, such as the popular 529 savings accounts. If you want to contribute to one of these programs, you are limited to the annual gift tax exclusion amount of $12,000. You could also give up to $60,000 and treat it as a gift made over a five-year period. The maximum allowed amount is $60,000, so you can give less if you wish. This tactic comes with a price, however. First, you cannot give the same beneficiary another $12,000 financial gift for five years. Also, if you die before the end of the five-year period, the portion of the contribution you didn't survive will be included in your estate for federal estate tax purposes. In other words, if you die one year after making the $60,000 gift, $48,000 will be included in your taxable estate.

Think you have the exclusions under control? Good, because just to confuse you, there is one more layer you need to comprehend before you can truly grasp the gift tax. If you give gifts beyond the $12,000 annual gift tax exclusion and the other unlimited exclusions, you will need to fill out Form 709 with the IRS. This notifies the IRS that you made a taxable gift. It doesn't, however, necessarily trigger a tax. Why? Because you also have a $1 million gift tax exemption in addition to all the other exemptions. Once you exceed the $1 million mark in gifts that fall outside the legal exceptions, you will be taxed.

In other words, you can give your only son a $550,000 home and still not trigger a gift tax if it's your first large financial gift and it falls outside the rules for unlimited gifts (it's not to a spouse, a charity, or for tuition or medical expenses). Give away two such homes, however, and you'll find yourself in gift tax territory because you will have exceeded the $1 million exemption amount by $88,000 ($1.1 million minus the $1 million gift tax exemption minus the $12,000 annual exclusion).

TECH TALK: What counts as a gift? The IRS has pretty strict rules about what it considers a gift for tax purposes. An IRS publication explaining the gift tax has this to say: "The gift tax is a tax on the transfer of property by one individual to another while receiving nothing, or less than full value, in return. The tax applies whether the donor intends the transfer to be a gift or not." The IRS also makes clear that the tax will be imposed on any transfer of property when you give without expecting to receive something of at least equal value in return. In other words, don't try to get away with giving a gift under the pretense of making a sale. You cannot give your son a new car in exchange for $10 and call it a legitimate business transaction. According to the IRS rules, if you sell something at less than its full value, including an interest-free or reduced-interest loan, you are making a gift.

One more note about this $1 million gift tax exemption: The estate and gift taxes work in tandem as a unified transfer tax system. So when you use up your gift tax exemption, you are really using up your death tax exemption. It's known as the unified credit. The total amount of the credit used during life for gift tax purposes will reduce the credit available to use against your estate tax when you die.

The only problem is that the unified credit isn't really so unified anymore—not since the 2001 tax act. Before 2001, the unified credit amount applied to the gift tax and the estate tax was the same. Currently, $1 million in gifts is exempt from taxation. Meanwhile, the exemption amount for estate tax purposes is increasing.

Year	Applicable Exclusion for Gift Tax Purposes	Applicable Exclusion for Estate Tax Purposes
2005	$1 million	$1.5 million
2006	$1 million	$2 million
2007	$1 million	$2 million
2008	$1 million	$2 million
2009	$1 million	$3.5 million

How does this affect you? It means that you want to carefully juggle what you give away in life to avoid triggering a gift tax. Why? Well, if you give away $1.5 million now, you will be subject to a gift tax for the additional $500,000. Wait until you die, however, and you might be able to pass that additional $500,000 on tax-free, depending on the year of your death.

Gift taxes are a complex issue, but it's really something you need to worry about only if you're ever going to give away assets or property worth a substantial amount of money. Also, states generally don't tax gifts—that, at least, can be one less thing to worry about. (Some states, such as Connecticut, do impose a separate gift tax, however. You want to be aware of your state's rules before proceeding.)

Generation-Skipping Transfer Tax

It might seem hard to believe, but there is one more tax to consider. (Hang in there. I'll make this brief.) If you leave your money to your grandkids—or anyone of that generation—you risk being subject to the generation-skipping transfer tax. As the name implies, it's a tax imposed on wealth transfers that skip a generation—whether made in life or at death. The reason for this tax can be both perplexing and amusing. Think of it this way: If you were to pass $10 million to your kids, you would be taxed on the amount of the transfer that exceeds your personal exemption. Assuming your kids manage their inheritance wisely and pass it to their kids, the money will be taxed again, and so on. If you bypass your kids, however, and pass that money directly to your grandchildren, you will, theoretically, also skip paying the taxes the government would have otherwise collected when your kids die.

The good news is that people can transfer assets to their grandchildren and others of that generation free of taxation up to a certain exemption amount. The generation-skipping transfer tax exemption currently equals the current personal exemption for estate tax purposes ($2 million until 2008, and $3.5 million in 2009). If gifts to grandchildren exceed the exemption, you will be taxed at the maximum estate tax rate for that year (45 percent between 2007 and 2009). Transfers that qualify for the annual gift tax exclusion amount of $12,000 per person are also exempt from this tax.

TECH TALK: Will the Estate Tax Be Repealed?

Currently, there's a debate raging over whether or not to permanently repeal the federal estate tax. In other words, should legislators pass a law to make it go away for good (or at least until the next group of legislators decide to revive it)?

As the law stands now, the estate tax will be repealed for one year in 2010, and then return to the pre-2001 schedule, allowing a personal exemption of $1 million.

Proponents of a permanent repeal say that death should not be a taxable event. In other words, you work hard for your money, and you should be allowed to give it to whomever you please when you die without the government taking a cut. Opponents say that the estate tax repeal is really just a tax cut for the rich.

If you think all rich people have joined forces to support the estate tax repeal, however, think again. A number of wealthy Americans, including Warren E. Buffett, George Soros, and the father of Microsoft founder Bill Gates, have petitioned Congress to fight the campaign for an estate tax repeal. They worry that a repeal will result in an increase in taxes on those less able to afford it, or a reduction of many of the nation's vital social programs, such as Medicare and Social Security. A repeal of the estate tax could also harm charitable giving, which is one of the few ways wealthy people can shelter their dollars from estate taxation, critics contend.

Investment guru Warren Buffett has taken a more philosophical approach to the estate tax. He worries that a repeal will lead to generations of trust-fund babies. The estate tax helps maintain a society based on merit rather than inheritance, he has said.

Regardless of what happens, you should be prepared for a change in the system. Some experts suspect a compromise will be made allowing a permanent exemption at a larger amount—say, $2.5 million or $3 million. Bills are already being proposed, which means that a change could occur soon.

GETTING THE MOST OF YOUR EXEMPTIONS AND DEDUCTIONS

Now that you know all about estate taxes, it's time to learn about some common tactics for reducing your tax liability. Reducing your estate taxes is really just a matter of getting the most out of your various deductions and exemptions. Let's take a look at some common strategies for making the most of various exemptions and deductions to reduce your potential tax liability.

I-Love-You Will: How Relying Too Heavily on the Marital Deduction Can Be a Mistake

The marital deduction can be a great tax savings tool. It essentially amounts to this: No matter how rich you are, you can avoid estate taxes by leaving everything to your spouse. Bill Gates, theoretically, could leave his entire fortune to his wife, Melinda, and be free of estate taxes. Professionals call this type of plan, where two spouses leave everything to each other, an "I-love-you will."

It's a romantic concept, but this seemingly sweet strategy can lead to a big tax trap. How? When you leave everything to your spouse, you give up your personal exemption. Then, when your spouse transfers that money to your children or other non-spousal heirs, there's only one exemption left to reduce estate taxes. By not using your personal exemption, you could create a bigger tax liability for your heirs.

Consider this theoretical scenario: Aruna and Kusumita are a married couple who share everything. As such, they each own half of a $2 million estate, or $1 million each. They both draft wills that leave everything to each other. The surviving spouse will then leave the combined estate to their son and daughter-in-law.

When Aruna dies, he leaves Kusumita his $1 million and owes nothing in estate taxes because the entire transfer is shielded under the marital deduction. When Kusumita dies several years later, she plans to leave the total $2 million to her son and his wife as planned. But Kusumita's only tax shield is her personal exemption, which isn't as all-encompassing as the marital deduction. If she dies in 2011, she would be able to shelter only $1 million from the federal government, leaving $1 million to be taxed. Even if she dies in 2009, when the personal exemption is $3.5 million, her transfer could be subject to state estate taxes depending on where she lives.

So what's the solution? Any couples with a combined estate that exceeds the personal exemption amount should consider what's known as a credit shelter trust, also known as a bypass trust or AB trust in some cases. With this type of trust, each spouse would leave his or her share of assets (often only up to the personal exemption amount) in a trust. When the first spouse dies, the second spouse is able to live off the interest of the deceased spouse's trust assets. The surviving spouse can also tap into the principal for medical or other emergencies. Yet the trust assets are technically not a part of the surviving spouse's estate.

As such, the money in the trust can't be sheltered from taxation by the marital deduction. Instead, it will be shielded from taxation by the personal exemption amount, which is why you generally want to fund it with no more than the exemption amount.

The surviving spouse retains his or her own assets separately. This way, when the combined estate passes down to the final beneficiaries, it benefits from two personal exemptions—always more powerful than one.

Let's take another look at Aruna and Kusumita, but assuming they used a credit shelter trust. Aruna's $1 million passes to the trust and does so free of estate taxes—due to his personal exemption, however, and not because of the marital deduction. Kusumita, meanwhile, still has access to her $1 million. Plus, she has been given rights to use the interest from Aruna's trust for her lifetime. Ultimately, however, the property is her son and daughter-in-law's. This way, when Kusumita dies, her son will receive her $1 million free of estate tax and his father's $1 million free of estate tax.

This type of trust setup is a nice solution for older couples since the possibility that the combined estate will remain intact is greater the shorter the surviving spouse's life expectancy. If your spouse is young, however, you may end up doing him or her a disservice by tying up the funds in a trust.

There are other risks to this setup, depending on how much money you have and who owns what. In our scenario with Aruna and Kusumita, each owned a clean $1 million. Thus, they could each devote their entire estate to a trust for the other's benefit without concern that the other wouldn't have enough money to live on. In real life, however, the numbers are rarely so clean. Often, one spouse has the majority of the money, or at least an amount that's potentially above the annual exemption amount. Determining how much to place in a trust thus requires more consideration.

Suppose you have $3 million and your spouse has very little savings. If you put the entire $3 million in a credit shelter trust, you run into two problems. First, you risk leaving your spouse without enough to live on, since he or she may have access only to the interest from the trust. Second, you risk placing more than the applicable exemption amount in the trust, thus incurring a tax. Many estate planners will write these trusts so that no more than the applicable exemption amount is placed in the trust in order to avoid the second problem. This, however, just reintroduces the first problem. If you die in 2009 when the exemption amount is $3.5 million, your spouse gets nothing but the money in the trust. You risk leaving your spouse without access to any principal, only earnings from the trust.

Generally speaking, people with a lot of money want to place only a portion of their estate in the credit shelter trust and then give the remaining amount to the spouse, either as an outright gift or through another marital trust. This way, you take advantage of both the personal exemption and the marital deduction. Plus, you ensure that your spouse is well taken care of.

One common technique is to use a combination credit shelter trust and so-called qualified terminal interest property (QTIP) trust. A QTIP trust gives the spouse access to interest from the credit shelter trust and, potentially, the principal from the QTIP trust. The benefit, much like the bypass trust, is that the donor can determine who receives the remaining QTIP assets when the primary beneficiary dies.

Let's take a hypothetical situation: Ralph and Alice are married, but it's a second marriage for them both. They each also have children from their first marriage. Alice is the rich one. Her estate totals about $4 million. Ralph has some savings, but not much. In order to continue his lifestyle if Alice were to die first, he needs access to her money. Alice wants to provide for Ralph, but she also wants to ensure that her children receive whatever inheritance remains when Ralph dies. Therefore, she cannot give Ralph any of the money as an outright gift. Meanwhile, she's also concerned about taxes, since she has a $4 million estate. Ultimately, Alice needs to meet three goals: to provide for Ralph; to pass the remaining estate to her children; and to avoid estate taxes.

To meet these three goals, Alice could just use a QTIP trust. Her entire $4 million estate would pass to Ralph. He would have access to the interest in the trust and potentially some principal. Alice can structure this any way she wants, so she might allow Ralph to tap the principal only for medical needs or for basic food and shelter, for example. With a QTIP, she has a lot of flexibility to structure the distributions as she pleases (so long as Ralph has access to the interest of the trust). With a QTIP, Alice can also name the final beneficiaries of the trust. Finally, she will avoid estate taxes, because the money that passes through a QTIP qualifies for the marital deduction. Thus, she can pass her entire estate free of taxation.

The downside to this scenario is that when Ralph dies, he will hand down a $4 million estate (assuming none of the principal was eaten away), all of which will be taxed on any amount above his personal exemption.

TECH TALK: On the surface, a credit shelter trust and QTIP trust may seem like they do the same thing. Indeed, they both allow you to put assets in a trust that will pay interest, and potentially some principal, to a spouse, all the while ensuring that whatever assets remain in the trust after the second spouse dies will pass to your intended beneficiaries. There are, however, some subtle differences between these two trusts. One of the main differences is in the way they are taxed. A credit shelter trust is taxed on the first death, which is why you want to fund it with your personal exemption amount. As such, the trust assets cannot be taxed again upon the second death. The QTIP trust, meanwhile, is what's known as a martial trust. As such, it qualifies for the marital deduction, and the trust assets are taxable on the second death. Also, while both allow you to pay the beneficiary income from the trust, there are some subtle differences in how you can structure payments that tap the principal.

A better solution would be for Alice to make use of both a credit shelter trust and a QTIP trust to more effectively reduce taxation on the second death. Since the exemption amount will hit $3.5 million in 2009, Alice might want to set a cap on the amount that passes to the credit shelter trust. If she passes on $3.5 million to the credit shelter trust in 2009, she risks leaving Ralph with just $500,000 in the QTIP. She might request that the amount of the exemption up to $2 million be passed into the credit shelter trust and the remaining assets be placed in the QTIP trust for Ralph's use. This way, as much as $2 million will be exempt from taxation on the second death. Only the money in the QTIP will be taxed if it exceeds Ralph's personal exemption amount.

So if Alice dies in 2006, $2 million will pass to the credit shelter trust and $2 million to the QTIP trust. The money in the credit shelter trust will be free of tax because the entire amount qualifies for her personal exemption, which is $2 million in 2006. The money in the QTIP trust is also free of taxation because it qualifies for the marital deduction. No matter when Ralph dies, the money in the credit shelter trust will pass free of taxes to Alice's children. Only the money in the QTIP trust will be subject to taxation if the remaining funds remain higher than Ralph's personal exemption. So if he dies in 2009, when the exemption rises to $3.5 million, the money in the QTIP will pass free of taxes. If he dies in 2011, however, when the exemption returns to $1 million, as much as $1 million may be taxed. Still, this is better than if Alice had placed the whole $4 million in the QTIP trust, in which case as much as $3 million could be taxed on Ralph's death.

Giving to Charity

Giving to charity is another time-honored way to reduce your taxable estate. Again, you can give unlimited amounts to charity without incurring a gift tax. Plus, the gift will reduce your taxable estate. There are other tax benefits to giving to charity, including the ability to escape capital gains taxes when giving away highly appreciated assets and the ability to take a tax deduction in the year the gift is made. (The benefit that comes from helping society is assumed.)

Charitable trusts and annuities can also help reduce estate tax burdens. Since any gift to charity will reduce the size of your overall estate, you may be wondering why anyone would want to contribute to charity through the use of a complicated trust or annuity. These strategies are generally used to allow donors to simultaneously benefit from tax reductions that come from giving to charity while still retaining some control over the donated assets.

Let's take a close look at some of the tactics for giving to charity while generating a stream of income:

- *Charitable remainder trust:* A charitable remainder trust is an example of a trust that offers income benefits in addition to the tax benefits that come from giving to charity. You place money in the trust and the charity, normally, acts as trustee. However, you retain rights to some income from the trust, and the income beneficiary can be yourself, your spouse, a child—anyone you want. You can also determine the income-producing period. You might, for example, structure it so that your spouse receives $10,000 from the trust every year until he or she dies. Once your spouse dies, the remaining assets go to the charity. One major benefit of this type of trust is that you can contribute highly appreciated assets and not pay capital gains. Say, for example, that you purchased stock for $50,000 twenty years ago. Now it's worth $500,000. If you sold that stock, you would be subject to capital gains tax on $450,000. By placing the assets in the charitable remainder trust, you can sell the stock without the immediate tax penalty. You can also take a tax deduction for the charitable gift. The amount of deduction you get, however, will depend on the actual size of the gift minus the income distributions.

• *CRUTs and CRATs:* There are two main types of charitable remainder trusts: charitable remainder annuity trusts (CRATs) and charitable remainder unitrusts (CRUTs). It sounds complicated, but it's not. The main difference is in how the income is paid to the non-charitable entity, such as yourself or your spouse. With a CRAT, the amount of income paid is fixed. So if you ask for $10,000 a year for ten years, for example, that's what you'll get. With a CRUT, the amount of income paid will vary depending on the assets in the trust. You might, for example, ask for 5 percent a year for ten years. If the trust were worth $100,000 the first year, you would get $5,000. If it grew to $200,000, you would get $10,000.

• *Charitable gift annuities:* This type of gift operates much like a CRAT, but it's not done through a trust. For this reason, charitable gift annuities are considered easier for charities to operate, and so charities will generally agree to set them up with smaller donation amounts—often for as little as $10,000, compared with the $100,000 minimums usually required to set up CRATs and CRUTs. Essentially, you give money (including appreciated assets, such as stock) to charity, and the charity agrees to pay you a set amount of income for life. It works almost exactly like a commercially sold income annuity, which is an insurance product that works a bit like life insurance in reverse: You pay a lump sum up front in exchange for income payments for a set period, sometimes for life. The main difference between the charitable gift annuity and the commercially sold annuity is that you will probably get smaller income payments with the charitable one. However, you will also get a tax deduction for the charitable gift, and the gift reduces your taxable estate—plus you get to donate to charity. Anyone considering investing in an insurance annuity to supplement his or her retirement income should seriously consider a charitable annuity.

• *Life estate and gift annuities:* This is another twist on the popular charitable gift annuity, best suited for people with valuable homes but not a lot of cash. With a life and estate gift annuity, you can give away your home to charity, generate a stream of income from the gift, and continue to live in the home for life. The drawback is that these things are difficult to find. Indeed, most charities will accept real estate in exchange for income, but few will allow the donor to continue to live in the home. The reasons for this are economic. Few charities have the cash at hand to pay out income for a gift they have yet to receive. Charities that permit life and estate gift annuities tend to accept only very valuable homes in areas likely to continue to appreciate in value, thus increasing the likelihood that the charity will still come out ahead in the end.

Other Types of Trusts to Reduce Estate Taxes

• *Irrevocable life insurance trusts:* When you die, whatever life insurance proceeds are paid from policies you own will be considered part of your taxable estate. If you have a lot of life insurance, you risk pushing your estate into a taxable position, or into a higher tax bracket. Irrevocable life insurance trusts solve this problem because they place your policies in an irrevocable trust. As such, you are no longer the owner of the policy. This method has many drawbacks, however. It can create problems with paying premiums, for example: Since the policy is no longer yours, why would you pay the premiums? In order to pay premiums, you may have to gift them to the beneficiaries and hope that they use the money to keep the life insurance active. A better strategy might be to transfer ownership of your life insurance policy to someone else.

• *Grantor-retained annuity trusts (GRATs):* This is a trust instrument that can help you pass on to heirs assets that are expected to significantly appreciate in value without being taxed extra for the appreciation. To establish a GRAT, you would place assets in the trust and establish a stream of income from the trust for yourself for a set number of years. The value of the GRAT will be established as a gift tax when you set up the trust. When the assets are distributed, whatever is remaining in the trust will be passed on to your heirs, free of any additional tax. So if the assets appreciate as you expected, you are able to pass on more than the taxable value of the trust. Another form of the GRAT is the grantor-retained unitrust (GRUT), which works similarly to the GRAT—with one major exception. The income payments aren't set, as with a GRAT. Rather, they are based on the annual value of the trust.

PART III

WRAPPING THINGS UP

Once you create your big-picture inheritance plan, you need to consider the details required to implement it. Consider it the "who and where" section of your plan: Who are you going to put in charge of the various aspects of your plan, and where are you going to keep your documents for safekeeping?

Previous sections of this book focused more on the "what and how" of the plan. What are your estate planning needs and how might you best meet those needs? This section will help you answer questions such as: *Do I need a lawyer? If yes, how do I find one? Do I need to hire a professional trustee or money manager? Where am I going to store my documents so that they're safe? What do I do if I need to make changes?*

In this section, I'll also discuss how you can direct your own final arrangements. This is perhaps one of the most self-indulgent aspects of estate planning. Your final arrangements are all about you. You decide how you want your body to be disposed of and how you want your life commemorated. You decide what flowers you want displayed or what songs you want played. These final acts often symbolize who we are and what we value. It's your final good-bye to the world. After all this tough planning to make sure your family is taken care of, the final arrangements are something for yourself. Make sure to take the time to do it your way.

CHAPTER 15

IF NOT YOU, THEN WHO?

A PLAN IS ONLY AS GOOD AS THE PERSON IN CHARGE

Poor leadership can ruin even the most perfect of plans. This couldn't be more true than when it comes to estate planning. If you want things to go smoothly for your heirs, you need to choose the right people to carry out your wishes.

There are five main positions that may need to be filled when it comes to estate planning: the executor, the trustee, the attorney-in-fact, the health care proxy, and the guardian. If you have an ongoing trust, you also want to consider some auxiliary positions, including trust protector and asset manager.

You may find that you need only one or two of these positions filled. It depends on your plan. Someone with a simple will, for example, wouldn't need a trustee or a trust protector—just as someone without young children wouldn't need to find a guardian. However, you will no doubt require at least one of these positions filled.

Choosing someone to fill these positions can be quite easy

when you have someone close to you whom you trust. Most people, for this very reason, turn first to their spouse or an adult child to take on one or more of these roles. Generally, any beneficiary will work out just fine. Still, you want to be aware of hidden traps that can meddle with your plans.

When Elaine's aunt wrote her will, she did what many people do when choosing an executor: She chose one of the beneficiaries. She decided upon the beneficiary who was a professional accountant, assuming that he was best suited for the task.

What the deceased didn't anticipate, however, was how badly this beneficiary was going to react to his inheritance. Shortly before she died, Elaine's aunt had changed her will to give more to all the female heirs, who she believed were in greater need of the money. She, therefore, had less to give to all the male heirs, including the accountant. The accountant, who was also now the executor, did a shoddy job of administering the will. He even threatened a lawsuit and hired an attorney. Elaine and the other heirs eventually joined forces and hired their own attorney to help them get the estate settled, all of which cost money—some of it directly from the estate.

It's likely that the aunt never thought the executor, or anyone else for that matter, would get upset over the distribution. After all, she thought she was helping those who needed it most. This small oversight in human emotional reaction, however, cost everyone extra grief and money.

Here are some guidelines to remember when choosing the people to carry out your wishes when you die:

- *Clear your choice with that person:* Always get your nominee's approval. This may seem obvious, but it's not uncommon for people to keep their nominees in the dark. You should always clear your decision with the person of your choosing and give him or her time to think about it. The worst that can happen is that your choice will say no. And at least it will happen while you're still around to find a replacement.

- *Consider payment:* Many of these positions are paid positions. How much the executor gets may be regulated by state law, and may go up or down depending on the size of the estate. You can, of course, negotiate the fees paid as part of your plan. People who carry out your wishes who are also beneficiaries will often agree to waive the fee. People sometimes choose family members to do the job because they want to save money, and family is less likely to accept money to do the job. If the job is complex, however, consider encouraging the person taking on the job to accept some payment. It's only right that the trustee of an ongoing trust be able to receive a little bit of compensation for the work that's put into maintaining the trust, as well as the fiduciary responsibility the trustee accepts when taking the job.

- *Have a backup plan:* Always name a successor to take over if the person you name for the job is unavailable, unwilling, or unacceptable. This means having a successor executor, trustee, guardian, health care proxy, and attorney-in-fact. You want control over who takes care of your estate if the person you were relying on is suddenly unavailable.

- *Ensure cooperation:* You can often name more than one person for many of these positions, including co-executors and co-trustees. If you do, you will want to determine how decisions are made. Can the co-executors act independently or must they act as a group? You can also hire a professional to be executor or co-executor. Trust banks and lawyers will agree to do the job, but generally this is unnecessary and costly. Again, if the person you appoint needs help with the accounting or legal advice, he or she can simply hire someone to do these tasks.

• *Avoid conflicts:* One of the biggest mistakes people can make when choosing people to carry out their estate plan is to choose someone with pre-existing conflicts with their heirs, such as a stepmother or stepfather. Even if the person in charge is responsible enough to overlook past conflicts and do the right thing, your heirs might not be so kind. Try your best to choose someone without conflicts of interest. Naming a sibling to be the trustee of another sibling's trust may sound like a good idea on the surface, but it could encourage bitterness and rivalries.

CHOOSING AN EXECUTOR

The executor is often the most important position in settling an estate. Again, this is the person named in the will who is expected to carry out the terms of the will. A woman executor is also known as the executrix. Some states call the executor the personal representative.

When choosing someone to fill the executor role, you want to find, first and foremost, someone you trust to carry out your wishes and to do the right thing for you and your heirs. Because trust is such an important quality in an executor, most people look to a beneficiary of the estate—usually a close family member, such as a spouse or adult child. By choosing someone who stands to gain from the estate, you are choosing someone who is likely to take care of the assets and do a good job.

At the same time, you want someone with the patience and administrative skills required to implement the various steps along the way. Executing a will can be a tedious process, requiring filing of taxes and other unpleasant administrative duties. This doesn't mean you need to hire a professional, or appoint a beneficiary who is a lawyer or an accountant. Executors can always turn to professionals to fill in the gaps if they need legal advice or help with money management.

Still, this person should have the common sense to know whom to turn to for what, and the administrative skills required to meet deadlines and manage paperwork. It's also important that the executor be able to get along with your heirs, since he or she will be their main source of information about your estate. Your heirs will be upset about your death, and they may grow impatient, or even feel angry, about their inheritance. Good relations between the executor and heirs can help extinguish the small fires.

Your executor's duties will depend largely on the needs of your estate and the rules of the local probate court. A large estate with lots of feuding beneficiaries, for example, will be handled very differently from a small estate with one or two main beneficiaries. Still, there are some common elements to the settlement of almost all estates. Here are some of the executor's main duties:

- *Locate the will:* One of the first things your executor wants to do is locate your will. Hopefully you have left it in a safe place and told your executor its whereabouts the day you signed.

- *Identify, secure, and value all property:* The executor will also want to locate all your property to make sure it's safe and secure. If property needs to be managed—real estate, for instance—the executor should take the appropriate steps. He or she will also want to create an inventory of the property, including values. In some cases, professional appraisals must be ordered.

- *Post bond:* Your executor may need to post bond with the court, money that will be returned if the estate is properly settled. You can ask in your will that the bond be waived, a practice that is generally recommended for any trustworthy executor.

- *Notify heirs, creditors, and the general public of your death:* Your executor will also want to notify interested parties of your passing. This means notifying the beneficiaries named in your will, along with your legal heirs. It also means notifying your creditors. In addition to personal calls and letters, a death notice should be published in the local paper. Also, the executor should notify anyone doing business with the decedent, including the post office, utility companies, banks, and credit card companies.

- *Cancel any unnecessary ongoing costs:* This means canceling unnecessary insurance policies, magazine subscriptions, cable television, and the like.

- *Collect any income owed:* The executor should contact the decedent's employer and collect any unpaid salary or benefits, including pension and life insurance. He or she should also contact the necessary federal agencies, including the Social Security Administration or veterans associations, and check for any unpaid benefits.

- *Pay all expenses, debts, and taxes:* The executor will also want to pay any debts and taxes owed by the deceased, including outstanding utility bills and credit card debts.

- *Distribute the property to the heirs:* Your executor needs to supervise final distribution of assets to the heirs. Generally, this is done after all debts are paid and enough time has elapsed that no additional creditors can come after the assets in the estate. Receipts should be obtained.

- *Close the estate:* To close the estate, the executor will have to submit a report of his or her activities to the court. This report, often referred to as an accounting, should demonstrate that all debts have been paid, the assets were distributed to the beneficiaries, and all income to the estate was accounted for.

CHOOSING A GUARDIAN FOR MINOR CHILDREN

Choosing a guardian for minor children is a very different task from choosing an executor or trustee. This is the person you want to raise your children, so other skill sets will come into play, including lifestyle, value system, and temperament. In addition to choosing a guardian for your children, you need to decide whether this person will also manage your children's inheritance. If not, you want to choose a separate person to act as custodian over their inheritance. (See chapter 3 for more information.)

CHOOSING A HEALTH CARE PROXY

Your health care proxy is the person you want to make decisions about your medical needs if you are ever unable to do this yourself. It may be the same person as your executor or trustee, but this is also a very different role from many of the others involved in estate planning. Your health care proxy should be someone you trust with your life, not just your money. This person may ultimately decide whether to pull the plug and let you die or insist that you receive artificial life support indefinitely. Again, be aware of conflicts of interest. Someone who stands to inherit all your money, for example, may have an interest in letting you die. Of course, a living will can also help establish your wishes up front, thus limiting the health care proxy's authority. (See chapter 12 for more information.)

Choosing an Attorney-in-Fact

This is the person who has control over your finances, who can write checks or pay bills just as if he or she were you. Your attorney-in-fact may gain these powers immediately, or only for a set period of time—often only if you become incapacitated. Naturally, this must be someone you trust to do the right thing with your money even if you are incapacitated and unable to monitor his or her doings. (See chapter 12 for more information.)

Choosing a Trustee of a Living Trust

The living trust operates very similarly to a will in that the assets are passed to the intended beneficiaries after your death. Once the process is completed, the trust dissolves, much in the same way that the probate process ends after all the assets are successfully transferred. The point is this: The successor trustee to a living trust is similar to an executor of a will. Indeed, many people choose the executor to their will to also act as successor trustee to their trust; this is most commonly a spouse or adult child. Generally, you will be the initial trustee of your living trust, and your main beneficiary or beneficiaries will be the successor trustee(s). You want someone who can deal with the details and paperwork required to properly transfer the assets in the trust to the final beneficiaries. Also, this person should be able to manage your assets in the trust in case you should ever become incapacitated. (See chapter 8 for more information.)

Choosing a Trustee of an Ongoing Trust

It's more difficult to decide who to name as trustee of an ongoing trust, which can last for years or even generations. It depends largely on your goals. If the purpose of the ongoing trust is to protect an immature or incapable heir from squandering or mismanaging the money, you should name a third-party person to be the trustee when you die. This person would be responsible for managing the assets in the trust and doling out distributions, according to the language of the trust. This third-party person can be a close relative, a friend, or a professional, such as a trust company or an attorney.

If the purpose of the trust is accomplished regardless of who is named trustee, you might consider naming the main beneficiary the trustee. If you set up a QTIP trust with the goal of ensuring that the remaining assets are left to your children, perhaps you're perfectly comfortable naming your spouse as beneficiary. The purpose of the trust is, partly, to protect against the spouse diverting the assets from the intended beneficiaries, such as the children. That goal is accomplished, however, when you create the trust, as the spouse cannot divert the assets. Still, he or she can mismanage the trust or potentially spend down the assets. These are things you want to consider when establishing your trust and naming the trustee.

Consider a trust for a disabled child; you may feel confident leaving the trust in the hands of a sibling. Likewise, if the trust is for a spouse who has no concept of managing money, you may want to name an adult child who knows about your spouse's needs.

Be aware, however, of conflicts that can arise when you name one family member trustee over another family member's trust. Indeed, one of the biggest mistakes people make when setting up a trust is making one sibling trustee over another's trust. It can seem like a good idea on the surface. Say you establish a spendthrift trust for your son, Jabari. You may automatically think to name his sister, Rashida, trustee, because she is responsible with money and she is wise to Jabari's habit of "borrowing" money for frivolous things. This may all be true, but if you base your decision solely on these factors, then you're ignoring a very important element: the emotional factor.

Jabari may well feel resentment at the prospect of being treated like a baby, which is fine, except that he might also take that resentment out on his sister. He could harass her for money or even threaten her for not doing what he wants. Sometimes, these trustee–beneficiary situations can get violent. Even if Jabari behaves well, the setup could slowly erode their relationship. Every time they meet, Jabari will inevitably think about the inheritance that his sister is keeping from him.

WHAT ABOUT PAYING A PROFESSIONAL?

One big decision in designating a trustee is whether to use a family member or a professional. There are pros and cons to each choice, and you will want to weigh these factors against your personal circumstances.

- *Cost:* Family members are generally the better choice when it comes to cost. Family will generally help you keep costs low, often waiving fees, especially if they are also beneficiaries. Banks and other professionals, on the other hand, expect to be paid for their services. Trust companies tend to charge a percentage for assets-under-management, as well as a yearly administrative fee. These costs can be prohibitive to smaller estates. Indeed, some trust companies will refuse to manage trusts below a certain minimum. Before working with a trust company, you should ask for a schedule of fees and ascertain which services are included, and which are not, for the fees paid.
- *Mortality:* Trusts can last for many years, even generations. Human trustees can get sick, die, or simply become incapable of managing the trust due to adverse circumstances.

Professional trust services, on the other hand, offer less risk. If the bank merges, the new company automatically will take over the trust operations.

- *Expertise:* Since asset management is a full-time job for professional trust companies and banks, they should, theoretically, also be better than family members at the tasks required of trustees, such as money management. They're objective and regulated by law. Most trust companies maintain sophisticated methods; the same holds true for professionals who assist with other aspects of estate planning, like probate. Again, keep in mind that your choice of executor, trustee, or custodian can always hire a professional money manager, an attorney to help with probate, or even an accountant to help with taxes.

- *Personal touch:* No doubt, family members will be able to provide your beneficiaries with the personal touch they may require. Many people choose a family member to serve as executor, trustee, or other role, since he or she knows the needs of the beneficiaries. A trust company, bank, or attorney, on the other hand, can be a rather impersonal trustee, less willing to listen and discuss beneficiaries' needs or answer their questions. Beneficiaries may have to deal with different people at the trust company every time they call, since personnel can move around; the bank itself can also change hands, merge, or change locations. Still, while the impersonality of a professional trustee is generally considered a negative, it can be a positive when dealing with difficult beneficiaries. A beneficiary who wants more money might have the audacity to harass a family member, such as a sibling. Professional trustees, because they are so impersonal, are, theoretically at least, immune to tactics of manipulation.

Before you decide to put one family member in charge of another, you need to ask yourself whether you think there's room for abuse on either side. Here are some questions you should consider before naming family members as trustees:

- Will they keep the assets separate from their own?
- Will they keep good, clean records?
- Will they have the willpower to stay out of the funds in case of extreme financial hardship, such as unemployment or a child's medical emergency?
- Will they be able to deal with complaints or behavioral problems from beneficiaries?

An increasingly popular middle course between naming a professional or institution to handle these tasks and naming a family member is to name a combination of the two. You might name a relative as co-trustee and a trust company as the other co-trustee. This way, the trust company can manage the investment decisions and dole out the money according to the trust document, and the relative can be on hand to act as the personal contact for the beneficiaries. You can also name a relative trustee and hire a bank or investment company to manage the assets, thus redirecting a lot of the financial burden from the trustee. This could also help you lower costs, since the fee for investment advice can be smaller than the one charged to act as trustee.

CHAPTER 16

RECORD KEEPING

GET YOUR RECORDS IN ORDER OR
SOME ASSETS COULD BE LOST FOREVER

O nce you have completed your inheritance plan, you want to gather important records in a safe place. Keeping all your important documents together, accessible, and easy to find can help alleviate a lot of stress on your family after you die. Otherwise, your family will have to spend time going through files and tracking down your documents. That not only increases their burden and probably their stress, but could also slow their ability to close your estate and collect their inheritance.

In a worst-case scenario, important documents can be lost forever. Consider Olivier. When Olivier died, his family had no idea where to find his will. As such, whatever plans he made for the distribution of his assets after death were lost forever. Additionally, the family members' inability to locate the will pulled them into disputes with others who wanted to claim a share of the estate. How did this happen? Well, Olivier's executor had seen the will shortly after it was drafted and was vocal about what she saw:

Olivier, she said, had bequeathed a good part of his fortune to a school in his small European hometown. The school officials also came forward to claim a share of the fortune. The family protested and demanded that the estate be divided as if Olivier had no will at all.

Here's another danger of sloppy record keeping: Assets can get lost. When Sylvia's father died, she thought she had everything under control. As a financial professional, she knew how to execute an estate. She also knew where to look and who to call if her father's records weren't in order. Yet one day—shortly after her father died—a friend of her father's called to tell her that her father had taken out an insurance policy with a membership organization they both belonged to. Sylvia was shocked. "There was no trace of it anywhere," she said. Indeed, had it not been for this friendly phone call, she would never have known that the policy existed, and the money would have been lost.

WHAT DOCUMENTS SHOULD YOU HAVE TOGETHER?

You want to gather everything that's important to your estate plan and keep it all in a safe place. Obviously, this includes your will, living trust documents, living will, power of attorney, and health care proxy information. If you created an ongoing trust, you want those papers to be kept with everything else.

In addition to collecting the important estate planning documents, you want to provide thorough written documentation of your assets and other property. What do you own and where can all of it be found? Remember, not all assets are covered by the will, including certain retirement plans and insurance. Whom should your family contact to get a hold of these assets? Create a list of assets and property to keep along with your plan documents. This list will tell your executor what you own and whom to contact for more information, including names and phone numbers for banks, brokerage firms, mortgage companies, and any accountants or financial planners who are in your service.

Also, prepare a list of personal contacts, including the names and phone numbers of your beneficiaries and people you would like contacted about your funeral. This can include former colleagues or distant relatives.

If you have prepared written instructions for your funeral (which you should do), you can keep a copy of that information with everything else. Ideally, however, you should also provide a copy of your funeral instructions to your family and your executor so that they know how to handle the disposition of your body. The will is often examined only after the body has been disposed of, so any funeral instructions you keep with your will may not be found until after your body has already been buried. (See chapter 17 for more information.)

Your executor may also need the following information in order to settle the estate:

- Your full name.
- Your place of birth.
- Your date of birth.
- Your spouse's maiden name.
- Your Social Security number.
- Your current address.
- Your father's full name.
- Your mother's full name.
- Your military discharge papers.

You also want to provide your executor with the names and phone numbers of the attorneys, if any, who helped draft your estate planning documents.

Think of your executor, or whoever else will care for your estate, as a sort of babysitter for the estate. When you leave young children for an evening, you provide the babysitter with important contact names and numbers, along with general instructions for feeding the kids and putting them to bed. If a child requires special care, such as medication before bed, you would provide instructions on that as well. The same care and preparation should be offered to the babysitter of your estate.

Where Should You Store These Papers?

Any safe place can be used to store your estate planning documents, including a safe in your home or office. Even a filing cabinet can work, although you want to consider the potential impact a house fire or theft might have on documents stored in this fashion. A bank safe-deposit box will also work, except that you want to make sure ahead of time that your executor will have easy access to this box upon your death. In some states, for example, when a box owner dies, the bank will seal the box. In order to open it, the state department of taxation will be contacted and the contents of the box inventoried. Access to a safe-deposit box is easier, far easier, if it is jointly held—though that can be a risk, too, if both joint owners die at the same time. Ask your bank about local rules surrounding safe-deposit boxes upon the owner's death before you go this route.

Who Should Know Your Hiding Spot?

Before you lock these documents away, make certain that all the right people know their duties and have access to the documents that pertain to their duties. Your health care proxy, your doctor, and a local hospital should all have a copy of your living will and your health care directives, for example. Generally, copies of these forms can be relied upon as though they were the original. Your attorney-in-fact should also have your power-of-attorney documents; if you ever become incapacitated, he or she will need proof of this power to gain access to your assets.

You needn't provide copies of your will or living trust to your executor or successor trustee, but you definitely need to let them know where to access that paperwork.

Generally speaking you should provide your appointees with copies of your documents and keep the originals for yourself. The key word is *copies.* That means a copy of the signed original. Do not hand out signed copies, which will be considered duplicate originals. If you hand out duplicate originals, you will need to track down each one anytime you make an amendment to your estate plan. There are some exceptions to this rule, however, so you need to do your research. In order for your attorney-in-fact to have access to your assets, he or she will usually need an original or a duplicate original.

WHAT IF YOU WANT TO MAKE CHANGES?

After you've put your estate planning and other documents away, you might want to revisit your plan down the road to make changes. Revising the plan every now and again is natural, especially since the will "speaks" only after your passing. Just try to keep your changes and revisions to a minimum. Lots of little niggling changes could cause trouble down the road, especially if your documents become difficult to decipher. Also, you could be setting yourself up for disputes if you make too many changes, making yourself look unsure of what you really want or susceptible to outside influence.

Here are some reasons you might want to consider revising your estate planning documents:

• *You get married:* If you marry and fail to update your will, your spouse will be entitled to receive his or her spousal election, according to the laws of the state. This could result in your spouse getting too much or not enough when you die. It could also lead to your spouse getting assets you would have preferred to give to someone else.

• *You get divorced:* Every state reacts to divorce differently when it comes to estate plans. Some states will terminate a former spouse's inheritance rights in the event of a divorce. In other words, the will is treated as if the former spouse had died. In other states, the entire will may be revoked due to a divorce. In still others, divorce has no effect on the will. Even if a state revokes inheritance rights under a will, it may not have the same power when it comes to living trusts. No matter what your state laws are, it's always a good idea to revise your estate plan after a divorce to make clear that you want whatever assets were formerly bequeathed to the spouse to be bequeathed to someone else.

• *You have another child or adopt a child:* Most states will provide for a minor child who was forgotten in a will. Also, some states will ensure that a child who was not specifically disinherited receives an inheritance equal to the other children. Still, it's always wise to update your estate plan with the addition of a new beneficiary. Again, this means all your documents—not just your will.

• *A beneficiary dies:* If one of your beneficiaries dies, you may want to make separate arrangements for the property to go to someone else. You can also design your will to automatically distribute assets to other family members in the event that one of them dies. A will that uses the per stirpes method of dividing an estate, for example, would say that only the children of your deceased heir would receive that share of the estate, to be divided equally among them. Meanwhile, a per capita distribution would allow all the grandchildren to equally partake in the deceased beneficiary's inheritance. Your might say, for example: *I leave all my property in equal shares to my children who are still living at my death. If any of my children should pre-decease me, the living descendants of each deceased beneficiary shall take the share per stirpes.*

- *You lose or sell property:* Generally, you don't have to revise your estate planning documents if you lose or sell property. The beneficiary is simply out of luck. You may, however, want to revise your will or trust if the loss of an asset creates an unfair distribution. If you bequeathed your son your IRA and gave your house to your daughter, you could be creating problems for your children if you sell your house, move into an apartment, and fail to change your will.

- *You add new property:* If you acquire probate property of significant value, you probably want to revise your estate planning documents to ensure that it goes to the right person or people. This is especially true if you have a living trust. The trust should be designed to make this easy through a so-called trust schedule.

- *You move to a new state:* Your will should be valid if you move to a new state. You might, however, want to consider revising it to reflect the laws of your new state, especially if you have moved from a community property state to a common law state or vice versa. There might also be other niggling details you want to consider changing to reflect the rules of your new state. Some states, for example, will not allow nonresident executors or trustees. Also, you want to update your living will, health care proxies, and powers of attorney, since these documents can vary widely depending on the state. It's also important to note the number of witnesses necessary to ensure a valid will (a good reason to have three to begin with).

- *You want to change the executor, trustee, guardian, or attorney-in-fact:* If you want to change the person you've named as your executor, child's guardian, or other role, you should also change or amend your estate plan documents. Always name a successor to every appointment so that you don't have to revoke or amend your estate plan documents if your main appointment dies or becomes unable to take on the tasks at hand. As I noted previously, the legal saying is, "Better your second choice than some judge's first choice."

CHAPTER 17

CONTROLLING THE FUNERAL ARRANGEMENTS

YOUR FINAL GOOD-BYE

In addition to the traditional estate planning documents, such as the will, you also want to make sure your family knows about what arrangements to make for the disposition of your body and for services to commemorate your life. The first plan that needs to be executed after any death is one to dispose of the body. Providing your family with clear instructions on how to do this can help alleviate a lot of stress. The last thing any family wants as they are preparing a funeral for a loved one is doubt about whether their plans are what the deceased would have wanted.

Any plan you make should outline two things:

- How do you want your body disposed of?
- How do you want your life to be commemorated?

There are many possibilities for disposing of a body and commemorating a life, from a traditional burial and funeral to a cremation and memorial service. If you don't tell people what you want, it probably won't happen the way you hoped. Leaving written instructions that set forth what you want done and with whom, if anyone, you have already made arrangements is very important if you want your wishes to be fulfilled.

If you don't leave instructions, your next of kin will have complete control over the disposition of your body. If your next of kin is your spouse or a child, he or she may be able to accurately predict what you would have wanted. There's always a possibility, however, that your next of kin—say, a mother, a father, or a distant cousin—has no idea what you would want or doesn't approve of your wishes. Indeed, more and more people want to be cremated. Yet not everyone approves of this method, believing that the body should remain intact after death.

CAN I REALLY HAVE IT MY WAY?

The first step is to know what you want. Here are some of the most basic questions you will want to contend with as you plan:

- How do you want your family to dispose of your body?
- Do you plan to donate any organs to science?
- If you're cremated, what do you want done with your ashes?
- Do you want to pick out your own casket or burial plot?
- Do you want your body to be embalmed?
- What kind of gathering would you like for friends and family to remember your life?
- Do you want any special music played or flowers displayed at your funeral or memorial service?
- Do you want your funeral or memorial service to be held at a specific church, home, or synagogue?

- Do you want a specific religious leader to preside over the service?

Let's take a closer look at some of your options in three important categories: disposing of the body; commemorating the life; and products and services. Then I'll talk about the pros and cons of pre-paying for these products and services. Lastly, I'll tell you how you can ensure that your written instructions are followed after you die.

Disposing of the Body

- *Burial and entombment:* A burial is the process of placing the body in the ground and covering it with dirt. Entombment is the process of placing the body in a tomb. Either method requires the services of a cemetery, which can provide the burial plot and a tombstone or other marker or a tomb.
- *Cremation:* A cremation is a process of reducing the human body to bone fragments using high heat and flame. The end result looks like gray ashes and can be kept in a type of metal vase known as an urn. The urn can then be placed in a burial plot or kept at home. The ashes can also be scattered over private property. Cremation generally requires the services of a crematory, which may be owned by a funeral home. You may also need a casket for viewing purposes, which can also be sold by a funeral home.
- *Organ or body donation:* You can donate your organs or your whole body to science if you wish. If you donate just your organs, the body will generally be promptly returned to the family for burial or cremation. If, on the other hand, you donate the whole body, your family may lose its chance for a final viewing, since some programs require the body to be transferred immediately after death. A memorial service,

without the body, could be arranged, however. Plus, the school or medical center will generally cremate the body and return the ashes to the family within a year or two. If you want to donate your body, you have to find a donation program and sign a form. Your family will not be allowed to donate your body without your prior consent. Also, keep in mind that your body can be rejected for various reasons, including obesity or autopsy.

TECH TALK: Services to remember the deceased aren't affected by cremation or a traditional burial. They may be affected by a donation of the body to science. If the program requires that the body be transferred immediately, a viewing of the body may not be possible.

Commemorating the Life of the Deceased

• *Funeral service:* The funeral service is the traditional way of remembering the deceased by gathering around the body and viewing the corpse. A viewing is usually held at a funeral home, which also prepares the body and provides the casket (unless the family decides to keep the body at home). The services are sometimes continued at a church or other religious institution. Finally, friends and family can follow the hearse transporting the body to a cemetery for burial or to a crematory for cremation.

• *Home funeral:* Increasingly, people are taking it upon themselves to care for a loved one's corpse in their own home, including dressing the body, buying a casket for delivery at home, and transporting the body to the burial plot or crematory for cremation. This process is more time-consuming, but also less expensive and more personal. People involved in the so-called death care movement say that spending time with the body of a deceased loved one can help with the mourning process. If you are interested in home death care, look to the rules of your state. Generally, it can be done if you obtain authorization from the state registrar. You would also have to go about the process of getting a death certificate completed on your own—a process otherwise usually handled by the funeral home. This most likely requires coordinating efforts with the attending physician and the registrar.

• *Memorial service:* A memorial service is usually conducted without the body present. Friends and family can gather at a church, a home, or another familiar setting days or even weeks after the body has been buried.

• *A combination:* Some families find that it makes sense to plan a combination of funeral services and memorial. One scenario, for example, might involve a simple graveside service for the immediate family and a memorial service for a larger array of friends and family at a later date. This kind of scenario is often fitting for someone who has two communities; perhaps you live and work in one place but want to be buried with your family in your family plot in the town where you grew up.

TECH TALK: Proponents of funerals argue that a viewing of the body is important for closure. Without a glimpse of the corpse, survivors risk denying the death. Opponents of funeral services often argue that they are just a way for the funeral home to make money, requiring all the trappings of a fancy casket, preparation and dressing of the body for viewing, and rental of the funeral home for the viewing. Regardless of the services you choose, know that you can personalize the service according to your own religious or ethnic customs or family traditions. Photographs and speeches by loved ones can make the occasion special.

Products and Services

- *Caskets:* The casket is generally the most expensive item you'll buy if you're planning a traditional funeral with a viewing. The average casket will cost slightly more than $2,000. Caskets made of more valuable material, such as mahogany, bronze, or copper, can sell for as much as $10,000, according to the Federal Trade Commission. Traditionally, caskets have been available for sale only by funeral homes. Increasingly, third-party dealers and craftsmen are selling caskets online. If you choose to use a casket not provided by the funeral home, you want to get the funeral home's consent. The funeral home, however, cannot charge you a fee for using an outside casket. Also, make sure the provider is willing to deliver the casket to you or you will be responsible for picking it up.
- *Caskets for cremation:* If you plan to cremate the body, you can skip the casket—one reason why cremation is generally cheaper than a traditional burial. The body must be covered in something, but it can often be anything from an unfinished wood box to a pressboard container or even a canvas bag. If you want a public viewing, however, you will need a casket. You can always consider renting one, thus reducing the cost of having to buy a casket that will only be destroyed anyway.

- *Grave liners and burial vaults:* A grave liner is typically a reinforced concrete wall that's poured into the grave to prevent the ground from caving in around the casket. Most cemeteries will require that you pay for a grave liner along with a burial plot. You can also opt for a burial vault, a higher-end version of the grave liner that also comes at a greater cost.
- *Graveside service:* If you choose to have a service at the graveside to commemorate the deceased, you may be charged a graveside fee by the funeral home.
- *Optional services:* Much of what is provided by a funeral home are optional goods and services that you can pay for if you wish, but that are not required. If a funeral home tells you otherwise, you should report it to the FTC. These services include, but are not limited to, transporting the remains, preparing the body, use of the funeral home for a viewing, a ceremony or memorial service, use of equipment and staff for a graveside service, use of a hearse or limousine, a casket, and cremation.
- *Embalming:* This is a process used to treat the corpse to prevent decay. Generally speaking, embalming isn't required by law, but some funeral homes will require it if there's a public viewing. If you choose an immediate burial or cremation, embalming is unwarranted. There are some cases, however, in which the law will require embalming. If, for example, the body was not refrigerated for a certain amount of time or if the time of the burial or cremation is far off, embalming might be required.
- *Basic services:* There is also a list of basic services that you have to pay for if you obtain help from a funeral home, according to the FTC. These include, but are not limited to, funeral planning, securing permits and copies

of death certificates, preparing death notices, sheltering the remains, and coordinating arrangements with a cemetery, crematory, or other third parties.

The average cost of a funeral, excluding cemetery costs, was $6,500 as of July 2004, according to the National Funeral Directors Association. Prices will vary depending on your location and the firm providing the goods and services. Be sure to shop around before you buy. FTC rules require funeral homes to provide prices over the phone, so you can start by calling a few homes in your area.

AVOID GETTING RIPPED OFF

Pre-paying for your funeral services or products, such as a casket, can be a very good idea. This way, you guarantee that you get what you want. Plus, you save your family members from the grief of having to shop around for the right funeral home or cemetery in the midst of their sorrow.

There are some risks to pre-paying, however. Here are some factors you want to consider before agreeing to turn over any money for funeral goods and services:

- What happens to your money if the firm goes out of business or is sold?
- Can you get a refund if you change your mind?
- If you move out of the area, how would your arrangements be affected?
- What happens to the interest on the funds if placed in an account?

Each state has its own laws on how a funeral home must manage money it receives for services in advance, but protections vary from state to state. Indeed, some states offer little or no effective protection, according to the FTC. In Florida, for example, you are entitled to a full refund of any money paid for services—but not for cemetery plots—if you change your mind down the road. Be sure to review your state's rules on funeral pre-payment before you follow through.

If you're uncomfortable pre-paying, you're not barred from pre-planning. You may be able to plan your funeral and keep your plan on file with a specific funeral home without putting any money down. You can then set aside money for the funeral in a money market or other interest-bearing account. The downside to this strategy is that costs for the products and services you choose could rise by the time you die.

Funeral insurance is another mechanism people look to when pre-paying funerals—but there are downsides to this method as well. If you skip a payment, for example, you could lose your coverage, leaving you with less money to pay for the funeral.

Enforcing Your Wishes

One of the biggest concerns people have when planning their own funeral is: *How can I be sure my wishes are carried out?* After all, what's the point of planning if you have no control over the end result?

Written funeral instructions may not be binding, depending on your state. Often, the next of kin is entitled to handle the deceased's funeral arrangements as he or she sees best. So long as you trust your family to carry out your wishes, however, this shouldn't be a problem. If you don't trust that your family will abide by your funeral wishes, you probably want to investigate what legal requirements exist that require your family or the funeral establishment to abide by your wishes.

Arizona, for example, has a statute that allows you to put your wishes in writing and requires that the crematory, cemetery, or funeral establishment follow those wishes. To make the document legal, you must be a legally competent adult. You also have to sign and date the document and have it notarized or witnessed in writing by at least one adult who is present at the time. Finally, you have to provide the crematory, cemetery, or funeral establishment with the funds necessary to pay for your services. In other words, don't plan for something you can't afford or your wishes won't be carried out.

Make sure to provide a copy of your written instructions to your executor and other family members. You can also keep a copy with your other estate planning documents. You can make your funeral wishes a part of your will, but this won't necessarily make them legally binding. Also, there's a risk to this tactic since estate planning documents are often reviewed only after the funeral; your plan could be overlooked.

CHAPTER 18

SEEKING ADVICE IN ALL THE WRONG PLACES

WHY YOU DON'T WANT A REAL ESTATE LAWYER TO DRAFT YOUR ESTATE PLAN

O ne of the first things people ask themselves when thinking about writing a will is: *Do I need to hire a lawyer?* The answer depends on what you want to accomplish and whether you have the confidence and time to do it on your own.

Generally speaking, there aren't many formalities associated with preparing a basic will. Even a basic living trust can be accomplished without the help of a lawyer. There are many books and so-called kits available that guide people through the process of writing a will or preparing a living trust. These kits, which can be purchased at any office supply store or bookstore, tend to contain basic will or trust documents. You just read the instructions and fill in the blanks. As long as your needs are relatively straightforward, these kits can meet your estate planning needs and save you some money in the process. Advanced computer software can also be had for a fraction of what even an hour's consultation with a seasoned legal professional would cost.

Still, there are some drawbacks to the do-it-yourself method that you want to consider before you jump in the car and run to your local office supply store or computer megamart. First, doing it yourself can take time. Sure, you can buy a will kit and fill out all the forms in one night, but you probably want to spend some time researching, talking to your heirs, and taking inventory of your assets to make sure you get it right the first time. Reading this book is definitely a good step, but if you plan to do it yourself, you want to do a bit more reading up on the subject. Also, you need to have the confidence that you can pull it off well. There's no sense in your second-guessing your work, staying up nights, and then finally bringing your will to a lawyer anyway because you worry that you got it wrong. Finally, seek out professional help if you have complex needs. A plan that involves multiple marriages, estate taxes, or ongoing trusts is probably best left to the pros.

Whom Can You Trust?

If you do decide to hire a lawyer, plan to shop around. Just as doctors have specialties, so, too, do lawyers. While any general practitioner can draft a will, you want someone who knows the process inside out—not someone who will spend his or her time looking up basic rules and regulations. Even worse, you don't want someone who will just pay for the same prefabricated form you could have gotten had you decided to do it yourself—and then charge you ten times the cost!

Jenny learned that specialty counts when she helped settle the estates of her aunt and uncle. When her uncle drafted his estate plan, he turned to the son of one of his golfing partners who was a real estate attorney—not an estate planning attorney. Despite this lawyer's focus on real estate law, he took Jenny's uncle's business and helped him and his wife draft their wills. They named Jenny their executor since they had no children of their own. Her uncle died first—sometime at the beginning of the year. Her aunt, meanwhile, seemed unable to take care of herself, so Jenny decided she wanted to be appointed her guardian. She turned to the attorney hired by her uncle, and he agreed to help her.

The whole process was a mess, she said. The lawyer didn't seem to know what he was doing. Bills went unpaid for months and the lawyer failed to warn Jenny about basic procedures, such as posting bonds with the court. Before Jenny was ever given a chance to act as her aunt's guardian, her aunt died. Jenny called the lawyer to ask about her aunt's will and he didn't even recall that he had possession of it, she said. He then failed to contact her for another month. Jenny had had enough and sought the aid of another attorney. Everything went much more smoothly. Still, she was left with feelings of guilt and frustration. She was angry with her uncle for not planning properly. Not only did he choose an inept lawyer, but he also failed to plan for many things, including the incapacity of his wife. She felt guilty, too, that she didn't seek out another lawyer sooner. If she had, she believes she may have gained guardianship over her aunt a lot sooner and perhaps could have helped her more in the last days of her life.

Finding the right lawyer is time-consuming, no doubt, but it will be worthwhile to take the time to shop around. You need to find someone who knows what he or she is doing, who will charge the right price, and with whom you get along. Of course, this is easier said than done. How do you really know whether the person you've chosen is right for the job until after the job has been accomplished? Likewise, how can you really get a handle on whether the cost is worthwhile if you've never done this before?

Resources to Help You Find Help

The first step is to try to narrow down your search by looking for lawyers in the right places. Here are some services you can turn to:

- *The American Bar Association* offers an online consumers' guide to hiring legal help. The site will help you research whether a person is licensed as a lawyer in your state and find out what you can do to deal with a troublesome attorney. It also offers information about free legal services for qualifying individuals. Go to http://www.abanet.org/legal services/findlegalhelp/home.cfm for more information.
- *The American College of Trust and Estate Counsel* is a membership association for lawyers who focus on wills, trusts, and estate planning. As such, it can provide a list of member lawyers, known as fellows of ACTEC, by state. More than twenty-three hundred ACTEC fellows are currently listed on the group's Web site, including telephone and e-mail. Go to http://www.actec.org/public/roster/search.asp for more information.
- *The National Association of Estate Planners & Councils* is another membership organization for professional estate planners. It also provides a list of its accredited estate planners. Go to http://www.naepc.org/ for more information.
- *AARP,* the association for people over fifty, can also help you find a lawyer. One potential benefit of the AARP service is that it has negotiated lower prices for members who consult participating attorneys. Go to http://www.aarp .org/families/legal_issues/ for more information.

TECH TALK: One neat trick to finding a lawyer is to call your local bar association for a referral. Local bar associations often have referral services that point you to a lawyer who specializes in your area of need, and allow you to pay for a consultation at a discounted price. In New York City, for example, you can get a thirty-minute consultation for $35 by going through the city bar association. If you like what you hear, you can negotiate the price for additional services. If you don't, the most you lose is $35.

Even estate planning specialists may have their own specialties within the field of estate planning. Sounds weird, right? In fact, it happens all the time. One lawyer may focus primarily on wills, living trusts, and probate proceedings, while another lawyer may focus on planning for elderly people who need to coordinate their estate planning with planning for Medicare. Before you choose an estate planning attorney, know his or her specialties. If you're young, you probably want to bypass the so-called elder law attorney and go for someone who writes basic wills and trusts.

Once you have homed in on a number of qualified lawyers in your state and your area of need, you want to either talk with these lawyers on the phone or set up an appointment to meet with them face-to-face. The point of this exercise is to get a sense of whether they will help you and what kind of fees they charge. You also want to get a sense of your rapport with them. If you don't like the way a particular attorney treats you, don't work with that person. Find someone else.

AFTERWORD

Sadly, the writing of this book was interrupted twice by death. The first was someone dear to me: my grandfather. The second was someone I didn't know, but her passing underscored the fact that unexpected death happens all the time.

This second death was of a young woman, Nancy, whose mother was on a plane from overseas to see her sick daughter in a hospital in New York City. Nancy, who worked and lived in New York, had cancer. A few short hours before the plane landed, however, Nancy passed away. Her mother was shocked and distraught. The police even got involved. They refused to let Nancy's mom stay in her daughter's empty apartment alone. Yet she knew no one in the area—her closest relatives, besides Nancy, were in Virginia. So a college friend of mine called me and asked if I could take care of her for one night. She knew Nancy's family.

It was the middle of the night, but I agreed. It's difficult to say no to someone who's just lost her only child. The commonality of death links us all.

Neither of us slept that night. Nancy's mom cried and paced until dawn. The next morning, I escorted her to the morgue to identify her daughter's body. She began to talk about getting Nancy's things in order. It was obvious to me that this was going to be tough. Not only was her daughter's passing totally unexpected, but the aftereffects had to be handled in a foreign country.

Nobody, except Nancy it seemed, was prepared for her passing. Had they been ready, her stricken mother would not have been taken into an unknown home in the middle of the night hours after her only child died—or accompanied to the morgue by a perfect stranger.

Meanwhile, the settling of the estate was the least of her problems. Nancy's mother was still reeling from the knowledge that she had arrived just moments too late to see her daughter alive one last time. *If only I had known,* she said again and again.

These experiences with death taught me two things. First, you can never really be prepared for death. No matter how sick or old people are when they die, their loved ones will still feel shock, sadness, and regret. Second, I learned that the little things really do matter when someone passes away.

Everything in this book is a little thing. Every seemingly irritating or daunting concept or procedure offers a way for you to take away a small bit of the sting and the pain that those you love will have to go through. Some will even offer you a way to speak to your loved ones after you have passed, giving them a glimpse of your last wishes. At the very least, you want to prevent those you love from having to struggle to settle your affairs as they grieve.

Of course, the most important thing you can do to prepare for death is live your life to the fullest and spend time with your loved ones. You want your family to remember your life, not your death—so live it well.

—Kaja Whitehouse

LIVING WILLS

Here is an example of a living will as provided by the state of Arizona.

Living Will

(Some general statements concerning your health care options are outlined below. If you agree with one of the statements, you should initial that statement. Read all of these statements carefully before you initial your selection. You can also write your own statement concerning life-sustaining treatment and other matters relating to your health care. You may initial any combination of paragraphs 1, 2, 3 and 4 but if you initial paragraph 5 the others should not be initialed.)

_____ 1. If I have a terminal condition I do not want my life to be prolonged and I do not want life-sustaining treatment, beyond comfort care, that would serve only to artificially delay the moment of my death.

_____ 2. If I am in a terminal condition or an irreversible

coma or a persistent vegetative state that my doctors reasonably feel to be irreversible or incurable, I do want the medical treatment necessary to provide care that would keep me comfortable, but I do not want the following:

_____ (a) Cardiopulmonary resuscitation, for example, the use of drugs, electric shock and artificial breathing.

_____ (b) Artificially administered food and fluids.

_____ (c) To be taken to a hospital if at all avoidable.

_____ 3. Notwithstanding my other directions, if I am known to be pregnant, I do not want life-sustaining treatment withheld or withdrawn if it is possible that the embryo/fetus will develop to the point of live birth with the continued application of life-sustaining treatment.

_____ 4. Notwithstanding my other directions I do want the use of all medical care necessary to treat my condition until my doctors reasonably conclude that my condition is terminal or is irreversible and incurable or I am in a persistent vegetative state.

_____ 5. I want my life to be prolonged to the greatest extent possible.

Other or Additional Statements of Desires

I have _____ I have not _____ attached additional special provisions or limitations to this document to be honored in the absence of my being able to give health care directions.

HEALTH CARE PROXIES

This is an example of a health care proxy form provided on the New York Department of Health's Web site.

Health Care Proxy

(1) I,_____

hereby appoint_____

(name, home address and telephone number)

_____

as my health care agent to make any and all health care decisions for me, except to the extent that I state otherwise. This proxy shall take effect only when and if I become unable to make my own health care decisions.

(2) Optional: Alternate Agent

If the person I appoint is unable, unwilling or unavailable to act as my health care agent, I hereby appoint

_____

(name, home address and telephone number)

_____

_____
as my health care agent to make any and all health care decisions for me, except to the extent that I state otherwise.

(3) Unless I revoke it or state an expiration date or circumstances under which it will expire, this proxy shall remain in effect indefinitely. *(Optional: If you want this proxy to expire, state the date or conditions here.)* This proxy shall expire *(specify date or conditions)*: _____

_____

_____

(4) Optional: I direct my health care agent to make health care decisions according to my wishes and limitations, as he or she knows or as stated below. *(If you want to limit your agent's authority to make health care decisions for you or to give specific instructions, you may state your wishes or limitations here.)* I direct my health care agent to make health care decisions in accordance with the following limitations and/or instructions *(attach additional pages as necessary)*:_____

_____

_____

In order for your agent to make health care decisions for you about artificial nutrition and hydration *(nourishment and water provided by feeding tube and intravenous line)*, your agent must reasonably know your wishes. You can either tell your agent what your wishes are or include them in this section. See instructions for sample language that you could use if you choose to include your wishes on this form, including your wishes about artificial nutrition and hydration.

(5) Your Identification *(please print)*

Your Name_____

Your Signature _____ Date_____

Your Address _____

(6) Optional: Organ and/or Tissue Donation

I hereby make an anatomical gift, to be effective upon my death, of:

(check any that apply)

❑ Any needed organs and/or tissues

❑ The following organs and/or tissues_____

_____

❑ Limitations_____

If you do not state your wishes or instructions about organ and/or tissue donation on this form, it will not be taken to mean that you do not wish to make a donation or prevent a person, who is otherwise authorized by law, to consent to a donation on your behalf.

Your Signature _____ Date_____

(7) Statement by Witnesses *(Witnesses must be 18 years of age or older and cannot be the health care agent or alternate.)*

I declare that the person who signed this document is personally known to me and appears to be of sound mind and acting of his or her own free will. He or she signed (or asked another to sign for him or her) this document in my presence.

Date_____Date_____

Name of Witness 1   Name of Witness 2
(print) _____*(print)* _____

Signature _____Signature _____

Address _____Address _____

_____   _____

State of New York
George E. Pataki, Governor
Department of Health
Antonia C. Novello, M.D., M.P.H., Dr.P.H., Commissioner
1430 12/01

INDEX

ABOUT THE AUTHOR

Kaja Whitehouse was born in New Jersey and graduated cum laude from Trinity College with a degree in English literature. She has worked as a reporter internationally, specifically in China, and is currently a columnist with Dow Jones Newswires. Her articles, focusing mainly on personal finance, appear regularly in *The Wall Street Journal* and other publications worldwide. She is working on a second book about funeral planning at her home in Manhattan's Upper West Side, where she resides with two cats and, at last count, an aquarium of 12 fish.